Medium Format Cameras

User's Guide to Buying and Shooting

Peter B. Williams

AMHERST MEDIA, INC. ■ BUFFALO, NY

Dedication:

This book is dedicated to my parents, friends, and family, who have supported me through the years and without whom this book would not have been possible, and in memory of Rhea, my golden retriever who passed away while I was working on this book. It was a photograph of her taken with an old Rolleicord which helped fuel my interest in medium format photography and introduced me to the exceptional images provided by the format.

Copyright ©2001 by Peter B. Williams.
All photographs by the author, unless otherwise noted.
All rights reserved.

Published by:
Amherst Media, Inc.
P.O. Box 586
Buffalo, N.Y. 14226
Fax: 716-874-4508
www.AmherstMediaInc.com

Publisher: Craig Alesse
Senior Editor/Production Manager: Michelle Perkins
Assistant Editor: Barbara A. Lynch-Johnt

ISBN: 1-58428-042-5
Library of Congress Card Catalog Number: 00-132625

Printed in the United States of America.
10 9 8 7 6 5 4 3 2 1

Notice of Disclaimer: The information contained in this book is based on the author's experience and opinions. The author and publisher will not be held liable for the use or misuse of the information in this book.

Table of Contents

Why Use Medium Format?

Medium format is perhaps the most misunderstood of all types of cameras, and listening to a definition certainly doesn't help matters. By definition, any camera that takes film larger in size than 35mm, but smaller than large format cameras using sheet film is medium format. While this is technically the truth, medium format is better defined as those cameras that take readily available film larger than 35mm but smaller than large format sheet film. In other words, cameras that use 120 or 220 size film. However, this still doesn't get to the heart of the matter—what is medium format, and why would anyone want to use it?

Medium format offers a compromise between the lightweight and easy to use 35mm cameras, and the complete control and unparalleled quality of large format cameras. By using film formats whose negative sizes are at least 2.7 times larger than that of standard 35mm negatives, medium format images have less apparent grain and far greater detail than that of even the best 35mm negatives when printed the same size. To give you a better understanding of why this is the case, imagine taking a photo with a 35mm camera and then a 6x7 medium format camera, using the exact same film in each camera. If you make a print that is enlarged approximately 13.5 times the original negative size, you would obtain a 3½"x5" print from the 35mm camera, but an 8"x12" print from the 6x7 negative—with both prints exhibiting the same amount of apparent grain. To get an 8"x12" print from 35mm, you have to enlarge the negative 71.5 times its original size. In the process, you lose a great deal of detail and have far greater apparent grain in the photograph when compared to the 8"x12" from a 6x7 negative. Because medium format negatives require less

enlargement, you can often use higher speed films and still obtain better prints than a 35mm camera with the sharpest lenses and finest grain films.

When comparing medium format to large format cameras, the difference is clear. While a 645 negative (taking its name from its dimensions—roughly 6cm x 4.5cm) is 2.7 times larger than a 35mm negative, a 4x5 negative is 2.9 times larger than a 6x7 negative and 4.9 times larger than a 645 negative. This leaves large format the undisputed king of image quality, particularly when you consider that a common large format size is 8"x10" (four times larger than 4x5, thirteen times larger than 6x7, and a whopping sixty times larger than a 35mm negative).

"...what is medium format, and why would anyone want to use it?"

However, as many photographers have found, negative size doesn't mean anything unless you can get the shot. In this regard, large format loses when compared to medium format, and even 35mm. Because of the size of the equipment, large format cameras just aren't suitable for any sort of action photography and are difficult to use in the field. In large format, hand-held shots aren't easy or accurate—even with old press cameras. Medium format cameras, on the other hand, can often be used hand-held and are appropriate for field use.

Film expense is also an issue. 4x5 film often costs $2–3 per sheet, whereas $5 will buy you a roll of film for 35mm or medium format. And while a 4x5 negative has significantly better quality than a medium format negative, advances in film technology in the last few decades has narrowed the gap. 35mm still cannot rival the quality of medium format, but medium format negatives can often rival large format in prints enlargements of 11"x14" or less. Even at enlargements of 16"x20" or 20"x30", the quality of medium format is excellent, even from the "smallest" 645 negatives.

As a result, medium format has a great deal to offer simply in the quality of the negative and the portability of the equipment.

☐ Format Selection: Advantages and Drawbacks

The most important question remains unanswered, however. For what types of photography is medium format best suited? Since no format or camera is best suited to every type of photography, the best way to answer this question is to take a look at each individual format and its best uses.

35mm Photography. With lenses ranging from Nikon's 6mm fisheye through Canon's 1200mm f5.6L super telephoto (priced at $80,000) and the widest selection of film emulsions, 35mm offers the

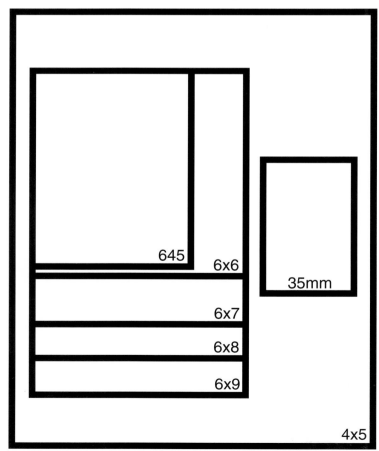

Precise negative sizes for common film formats.

greatest versatility of all formats. There's no type of photography the 35mm format can't be used for, and in the case of ultra–wide-angle and super-telephoto work, no other format even has the equipment available. The cameras are also relatively small and easy to work with, and offer the latest in technology, such as complex multi-segment meters, autofocus, and autoexposure. Using fine-grained film, decent 8"x10" or 11"x14" prints can be obtained, making it a popular choice with everyone from snapshooters through professionals.

Given such versatility, why even bother with any other equipment? As outlined earlier, the answer is quality. While the 35mm format can provide an acceptable print, there is still a significant difference between an acceptable print and an excellent print. Medium and large format are infinitely more capable of producing excellent prints than the small 35mm negatives. As a result, 35mm is far more limited than it would appear at first glance.

35mm is best suited for situations where smaller equipment gives you an edge in following and capturing the action. Likewise, any situation where you prefer to keep the size and weight of your camera to a minimum (such as when traveling), is also well suited to 35mm equipment. Particular types of photography, such as telephoto work or ultra–wide-angle photography, are also within the realm of 35mm, since medium and large format cameras have extremely limited offerings in these areas.

Where 35mm loses its edge is in any situation where fast action is not an issue. Landscapes, portraiture, and studio work can all be done with 35mm, but just as easily with medium or large format. And in situations such as these, medium and large format offer better options due to increased negative size and the resulting increase in final image quality.

As a general rule, 35mm cameras and other small formats (APS, 110, etc.) are best suited to situations where fast action or size of equipment is a significant factor. In more general situations, take Ansel Adams' advice and use the largest format camera possible to maximize the quality of the final print.

Large Format. The undisputed king of quality, large format, presents no compromises where the negative is concerned. Not only do you have

Show me the money! 35mm (left) vs. 645 (center) vs. 4x5(right). Each photo was taken with a standard lens for each format, photographed on T-Max 400 film with the exact same exposure time and lighting, and then printed on the same paper by a local professional lab. Great care was taken to make sure the negative for each format was correctly aligned and then enlarged to produce prints exactly the same size. The results are quite telling—35mm simply falls apart at large enlargements, while medium format retains good detail. Large format (4x5 in this case) reveals the absolute highest quality, as expected, but the medium format shot is still quite good. These photos represent approximately what you would see in a 20"x30" enlargement in terms of grain and detail from each format. Also note that I gave 35mm a true fighting chance—I chose 645 as the representative for medium format, the smallest negative size in medium format. Results from a 6x7 or 6x9camera would certainly have been much better than my 645 image, and truly embarrassed 35mm while knocking on the door of 4x5. The fact that the difference between 35mm and 645 is so telling despite using the smallest of medium formats speaks volumes to the potential quality any medium format negative can offer a photographer.

the largest negatives to work with, but you also gain tremendous control over perspective and depth of field. Even the old press cameras, such as the Speed Graphic, offer certain limited movements, while view cameras offer complete control with generous rise, fall, tilt, and shift on both the front and rear of the camera. For those demanding uncompromising quality and control, large format offers the best option.

Large format excels in any situation where time is not of the essence and you require absolute control over perspective. Architectural photography, for example, is an area where no other type of camera can match the results of large format. Even with the perspective-control lenses available for 35mm and medium format, large format offers greater range of movements and complete depth of field control. Your ability to adjust perspective is limited only by the image circle of the lens in use. This also makes large format the format of choice for studio photographers. In short, for any situation where you can take fifteen to twenty minutes to set up the shot, large format offers the highest quality option.

Where large format begins to lose its edge is in portability and ease of use. While some field cameras fold up into relatively small and light packages equivalent to a medium format rig, the actual movements of such a field camera are generally limited. For complete movements and perspective control, a view camera is required. However, view cameras tend to be large, heavy (between ten and twenty pounds is not uncommon for a modern view camera), and extremely slow to set up and work with. Thus, they are completely unsuitable for action photography, field work (unless you're young and don't mind carrying a lead weight on your back for hours), and not a good choice for general photography.

Film expense is also an issue. At $2–3 per exposure, film is expensive, and processing must be done at a custom lab capable of developing and printing large format negatives. As a result of the increased film and processing costs, large format can be an expensive proposition for amateur use. Those developing and printing their own black and white negatives may see only a moderate increase in cost, but anyone using color film in large format (both negative and positive), or those unable to process black and white themselves, will be stuck with high processing costs. As a result, large format is recommended for professionals who require the absolute best quality images for their clients, or amateurs who want the increased quality and can afford the added cost and weight.

Medium Format. As mentioned earlier, medium format fills the niche between 35mm and large format. Since the majority of medium format cameras available are completely manual, they are best suited to tasks where action is not a significant factor (although with the new autofocus 645 cameras, some medium format cameras can certainly be used in fast action situations). In general, in any situation where a manual focus 35mm camera can be used, a medium format camera could be substituted

and produce higher quality results. This makes medium format ideal for general photography, portraiture, and weddings, where the increased negative size provides significant increases in quality without sacrificing portability or ease of use (particularly when 220 film is used for increased number of exposures).

Because the majority of medium format equipment is designed for professional or serious amateur use, cameras and lenses tend to be of better quality. Unimpressive off-brand optics tend not to be available in medium format, because photographers using the equipment tend to be demanding of quality and unforgiving of inferior products. For those stepping up into medium format, this provides an advantage, since even the older, less expensive equipment usually offers excellent results.

Rhea Williams, 1995. Rolleicord V with Xenar lens.

☐ Basic Information

Negative	Area	Dimensions	x Larger than 35mm	Aspect Ratio
35mm	864mm²	(24x36)	—	1:1.5
645	2324mm²	(41.5x56)	2.7x	1:1.35
6x6	3136mm²	(56x56)	3.6x	1:1
6x7	3864mm²	(56x69)	4.5x	1:1.23
6x8	4368mm²	(56x78)	5x	1:1.4
4x5	11300mm²	(95x119)	13x	1:1.25

Print	Area	Aspect Ratio
5x7	22500mm²	1:1.4
8x10	51500mm²	1:1.25
8x12	61900mm²	1:1.5
11x11	78000mm²	1:1
11x14	99000mm²	1:1.27
16x20	206000mm²	1:1.25

Note: The exact ratio for specific film sizes is not exactly what is stated by the format. 6cm x 6cm cameras, for example, actually have an image size of 56mm x 56mm. Thus, I have calculated the aspect ratios based on the true film size. However, it should also be noted that, in some cases, the aspect ratio may not be correct due to variation in precise negative sizes from camera to camera. 645 cameras, for example, have negative sizes ranging from 41mm x 56mm to 43mm x 56mm. 6cm x 9cm cameras have actual negative sizes of 84mm x 56mm up to 88mm x 56mm. I have calculated the aspect ratio on the most common size for each format. For the exact negative size, consult the camera's instruction book or product literature from the manufacturer.

Another bonus the large number of serious photographers encounter using medium format is in processing. Medium format negatives tend to get more attention from processing labs because there is a higher likelihood that the images will be used professionally. This results in better quality developing and prints, even for amateurs shooting medium format just for fun.

Given this tendency towards serious use, one might expect medium format to be a more expensive proposition than 35mm. Quite the contrary—many excellent medium format cameras can be purchased for less than a new entry-level 35mm SLR, and there are a number of cameras taking 120 film available at insanely cheap prices. Old Kodak folding cameras, for example, can often be found for only $10–20. With a coated Anastigmat lens, these can provide amazingly good results for prints up to 11"x14". Other vintage folding cameras can be found in the $25–75 range with coated lenses, and film costs can be the same or less than 35mm. The Agfa Isolette, for example, has earned a solid following as it has a reasonably sharp lens. Like many of the old folding cameras, it makes an excellent compact carry-every-where camera, all for a cost of $50–75.

For this reason, medium format offers a certain fun-factor not available in other formats, as you can select and use a wide range of vintage equipment—much of which is unique in design and operation. And, because of the larger negative size, excellent 8"x10" or smaller prints can be made that simply overtake 35mm in detail and quality (particularly in black and white). For the photographer with a home darkroom, these vintage cameras offer a great deal.

Medium format can also be used for general purpose snapshots of family, friends, and vacations. The quality of the images will be noticed and appreciated by everyone. The photograph of Rhea, my golden retriever, taken in 1992 with a vintage Rolleicord V remains one of my family's favorite images of her. The incredible detail in the print not only shows the abilities of medium format to produce high quality images, but also how vintage equipment can produce such results. All in all, medium format represents an excellent choice for both amateur and professional photography, and is too often overlooked because of the mystique that surrounds medium and large format.

☐ Film Format Notations

In the interest of legibility, film formats other than 35mm will be discussed using their popular terminology, which drops the unit of measurement.

Therefore:

> 645 = 6cm x 4.5cm format
> 6x6 = 6cm x 6cm format
> 6x7 = 6cm x 7cm format
> 6x8 = 6cm x 8cm format
> 6x9 = 6cm x 9cm format
> 4x5 = 4" x 5" format

Chapter 1
Cameras, Lenses and Film

☐ Used and New Equipment

Cameras. When looking at camera equipment, there is a remarkable tendency for people to believe that because something is newer, it must be better. While there is a grain of truth to this statement, many photographers (particularly those with old Nikon or Pentax Spotmatics) can tell you that vintage equipment is certainly capable of excellent results, and often at a reduced cost.

In medium format, the large negative size can often reduce the difference between mediocre and top-notch equipment in enlargements of 8"x10" or less. With current manufacturers starting to increase the amount of plastic used in production of their cameras, many older cameras can be better bargains with higher construction quality (provided you don't need or want all the latest features). However, used equipment carries a greater risk of breaking, and you need to make sure you purchase equipment that is in good shape.

"Computer-aided design has taken lens design and manufacturing to greater heights."

In the end, the choice between new and used equipment is based on budget, individual needs, and willingness to take a risk on older equipment. Personally, the vast majority of my equipment is used, but I have also had to face occasional repair bills that likely would not have occurred had I purchased new equipment. With the wide range of excellent new and used medium format cameras available, concentrate more on choosing a camera that has the features to match your needs than on whether a specific camera is new or used.

Lenses. When considering lens performance, the old argument that newer is better finds stronger footing. Unlike camera bodies, where some of the old metal monsters will outlive most of the current plastic marvels, lenses have improved significantly in the last fifty years. When comparing lenses from the 1950s to those currently produced, the older lenses simply will not match the color, contrast, or sharpness of the modern lens, with only a few exceptions. In general, there seems to have been a significant improvement in quality every twenty years since the 1930s. First came the advent of lens coating in the 1950s, and then multicoating in the 1960s and 1970s. In the mid 1980s and 1990s, computer-aided design has taken lens design and manufacturing to even greater heights.

However, this amazing progression may appear to be for naught when you consider that a number of large format photographers use vintage lenses to produce astounding images, and some 8"x10" photographers even use lenses from the 1920s and 1930s to good effect. The paradox here results not from lens technology issues, but from film issues. As any 8"x10" photographer can tell you, vintage lenses are certainly not as sharp as modern lenses, yet they are able to produce high quality results because they use such large film. Because the film is larger, you don't need to enlarge as much, which reduces the chances of seeing problems such as lack of sharpness with a specific lens. Give a 1930s lens to a 35mm photographer, and he will likely complain of lack of sharpness, poor color, and overall unacceptable results—even in prints smaller than 5"x7". As smaller negatives are enlarged more at each given print size, abberations and flaws of a given lens are far more likely to become apparent. Thus, the larger the film

I took this snapshot (above) of the Flatirons with an old Super Ricohflex while hiking in Boulder, CO. I snapped it planning to crop down to the center section—partly for composition, and partly as a test of this cheap camera. The cropped portion of the photo (right) shows reasonable sharpness and resolution. This speaks volumes to the potential for using medium format, even if you use outdated equipment.

format, the less likely you are to see problems with a given lens. Black and white photographers also need not concern themselves as much with the color performance of a given lens, only the sharpness and contrast. Since contrast can be easily adjusted in the darkroom or in development, overall sharpness is the primary concern. This explains why many photographers using old lenses on medium and large format cameras can produce stunning black and white photographs despite the age of their equipment.

When considering medium format lenses, the overall performance of the lens is not as critical as with 35mm and other small format cameras, but at the same time, you can't get away with using early vintage equipment the way you sometimes can in large format. Again, medium format presents a compromise between 35mm and large format.

When looking for a good medium format lens, it is important to select one that is coated and of relatively good design. While multicoated lenses are definitely preferred, older single-coated optics are still quite good, with better lenses comprised of at least

four elements. To find out how many elements a lens has, hold the shutter open at the "bulb" setting, and count the number of reflections in the glass. Each reflection will represent one element. While this is not a foolproof method, it will give you a good idea of the number of elements. Coated three-element lenses are often found on older folding cameras, and can provide decent performance, provided you don't make enlargements over 8"x10" and don't mind slightly soft images.

For good color performance, a coated lens that is manufactured by a well-known company (Zeiss, Schneider-Kreuznach, Mamiya, etc.) is highly recommended, although preference is given in this regard to more modern lenses. In general, modern lenses produced for current medium format cameras will provide consistently better overall resolution and performance than vintage lenses, and should be used if images are to be sold or published.

Name Brands. Many photographers seem to have an impression that certain brands are better than others, based on name alone. In the case of older equipment (items sold new at least twenty years ago), there is a certain truth to this. Hasselblad, for example, did offer an overall better system of cameras and lenses than other brands, and provided better support. However, today's world is far different.

Since they have all switched to computer-designed lenses, the image quality of lenses from current major manufacturers is truly excellent. Modern production methods have also increased the quality of cameras produced, so that it is difficult to state definitively that one brand is absolutely more reliable than another. Each system works well, and repair technicians say that most brands are reasonably similar in terms of reliability and how frequently they see certain cameras for repairs.

In medium format, the lines between "old and new" and "good and bad" are even more blurred. Since you are using a larger negative, differences between lenses and equipment often do not become apparent until you make enlargements over 11"x14". If you were to take the same picture with a modern Hasselblad, an older Kowa Six, and an old Bronica S2A, most observers would be hard-pressed to tell the difference between the final images at common print sizes (11"x14" or smaller). Thus, you can often use older equipment and still achieve top-notch results. This is one reason why large format photographers can often use vintage lenses and still produce images that blow away all smaller formats, particularly in black and white. Consider the fact that many of Ansel Adams' early prints were taken with very early optics, but because he used 8"x10" film and did a large number of contact prints, the quality of the images is astounding. This is also why photographers using vintage Rolleiflex TLRs still produce such wonderful images.

So when considering a medium format camera or system, don't rely unconditionally on the brand name. Pay more attention to the

(Top) Camera: Bronica ETRSi with 50mm lens. Note the obvious wide-angle perspective from using a 50mm lens in medium format instead of the "normal" perspective that would have been expected from a 50mm lens on a 35mm camera. Because of the larger negative, a 50mm lens on a 645 or 6x6 camera will actually give you a view similar to a 30mm lens on a 35mm camera, hence the wide-angle perspective.

(Bottom) Hancock Shaker Village in Pittsfield, MA. Taken with my Bronica ETRSi and 75mm f2.8 PE lens, this photo reveals the detail and quality possible from today's computer-designed lenses featuring the latest multicoating.

features offered by the camera, and whether they fit your needs.

☐ Medium Format Lenses

Focal Length. When looking at larger format cameras, one difference that almost inevitably confuses people is that a 50mm lens on a 35mm camera is not the same as a 50mm lens on a medium format camera. While technically they are the same focal length, the lens 50mm on the 35mm camera will provide a "normal" view, while in the medium format, a 50mm provides a wide-angle view. The reason for this stems from the size of the negative. A 50mm lens only covers a 43mm diagonal on a 35mm negative, but must cover a 69mm diagonal for a 645 negative. As a result, the same focal length will provide an increasingly wider angle of view on the negative as film size is increased. How then, do you figure out what the lens in front of you does?

To get an idea of the angle of view and use for a particular lens, the easiest method is to convert the focal length into an equivalent lens in 35mm. First, choose the format you are interested in, and then multiply the focal length of the lens by the format's multiplier. For example, to figure out the 35mm equivalent of an 80mm lens on a 6cm x 6cm camera, multiply the focal length by .59 (the format's multiplier). This tells you that an 80mm lens on a 6cm x 6cm camera is roughly equivalent to a 47mm lens on a 35mm camera (80 x .59=47.2). For ease, round this off to 50mm, and you now know that an 80mm lens on a 6cm x 6cm camera will be roughly equivalent to using a 50mm lens on a 35mm camera.

In general, the normal lens (equivalent to a 45–55mm lens in 35mm terms) for a given format

☐ Image Circle

It should be noted that the diagonal of the film also provides the required image circle of a lens for a given format. For example, a lens designed with a 45mm image circle would be ideal for 35mm, but completely useless for medium format photography, as a 645 negative requires a 69mm image circle to cover the entire image area without vignetting. For the most part, image circle is not important to note unless you use a view camera and need to know how much room you have for movements with a given lens.

☐ Format Multipliers

Use these numbers to convert medium format focal lengths to the equivalent 35mm focal length.

FORMAT:	MULTIPLIER:
35mm	1.00
645/6x6	0.59
6x7	0.54
6x9	0.5
4x5	0.3

☐ Type of Lens

Once you have converted the medium format focal length to its equivalent 35mm focal length, use the chart below to determine the type of lens.

35MM FOCAL LENGTH	TYPE OF LENS
24mm or less	Ultrawide
35mm or less	Wide Angle
45-55mm	Normal
85-135mm	Short Telephoto
135-180mm	Medium Telephoto
200mm +	Long Telephoto

will be equal to the diagonal of the film. For 6x6, the diagonal is 81mm, for 6x7 it is 88mm, and for 6x9 it is 104mm. Thus, the normal lenses for these formats are generally considered to be 80mm, 90mm, and 105mm respectively. Because the film formats vary in aspect ratio, it is difficult to give an exact equivalent to a 35mm camera lens. The format multipliers will, however, provide a good general guide.

Lens Coating. When light passes through a lens, not all of it actually makes it through to the film. Some light will be absorbed by the glass, and some will be reflected off the surface of each element. Additionally, since different colors travel at different speeds (wavelengths), they can separate when passing through a slow medium (such as a glass element), causing what is called chromatic aberration. As you might imagine, all these problems have detrimental effects on the final image. Absorption of light by the glass elements will reduce the amount of light striking the film, lowering the effective aperture of the lens. Reflections off the surface of each glass/air surface further reduces the effective aperture of the lens, and also introduces serious problems such as flare

15

and ghosting. Separation of colors as they pass through the glass elements means that each color will not focus at the same point, which will reduce color and sharpness in the negative.

(Top) Taylor Hall at the Loomis Chaffee School in Windsor, CT. Taken with a single-coated Schneider Xenar lens, note that flare in this photo is very well controlled, and both contrast and detail are excellent. The blown-out highlights in some of the windows result not from the lack of multicoating, but from the long exposure time. Very few lenses, modern or vintage, could have performed better in this situation, given the long exposure time.

(Bottom)Hancock Shaker Village, Pittsfield, MA. While the bright window and reflection off the floor could have caused some older uncoated lenses flare or ghosting problems, the 75mm PE lens on my Bronica ETRSi handled the situation flawlessly. The lens also shows exceptional clarity and contrast, as expected from a modern computer-designed lens.

Take a look at light passed through a prism. Just as the prism separates light into the colors of the rainbow, each glass element in your lens does the same—to a lesser degree. Since absorption of light by individual glass elements is a factor of the glass itself, lens coating addresses the other issues—internal reflections, flare, and the separation of colors as they pass through each element.

The main advantage of lens coating is light transmittance. Even simple single coating permits 90–95% or more of light to travel through each lens element rather than be reflected off the surface of the element, thus greatly reducing flare and light loss. Multiple lens coating (generally known as multicoating) improves transmittance to 97–99.9%, depending on the manufacturer's formula and coating process. This offers even greater reductions in flare. As flare can also lower contrast, lens coatings also increase contrast and color simply because of the increased transmittance and reduced flare. In terms of color, contrast, and overall resolution, this factor alone makes a tremendous difference between a standard glass lens and a coated version of the same lens.

The separation of individual colors as light travels through the glass presents a much more difficult problem to tackle, yet both single- and multicoatings make some correction to keep colors together so they all focus properly at the film plane. As you might have guessed, this process is extremely difficult, and to fully correct a lens, you need more than multicoating. Special glass types, aspherical elements, and extraordinarily precise design and manufacturing are all required—which is why the best modern lenses cost as much as they do.

For the majority of well-designed, 35mm, fixed–focal-length lenses (and many medium and large format lenses), merely adding single coating improved performance to such a degree that many

☐ Zoom Lenses

The largest beneficiary of multicoating was the zoom lens, because multicoating allowed designers to produce compact, multielement, wide-range zoom lenses for 35mm cameras.

classic lenses with only single-coating can come very close to matching the performance of modern lenses. Mamiya TLR lenses, for example, are only single-coated, yet still widely respected for their sharpness, color, and overall resolution. Multicoating improved quality, but only the most discerning of observers can tell the difference between a photograph taken with a 1950s Rolleiflex and the latest Hasselblad CFi lens (except at extreme enlargements). Unless you make the most critical of judgements on your final images, constantly produce large enlargements, or plan to sell your images professionally, you will likely not see a tremendous difference between a well designed, single-coated lens (such as the Zeiss Tessar on early Rolleiflex TLR cameras) and the latest multicoated Hasselblad offering. As a result, don't get caught up in the multicoating hype. All modern lenses will be multicoated, and even slightly older single-coated optics can offer first-rate performance.

It is highly recommended that you make sure any medium format camera you buy has a coated lens, whether single or multi. Improved color performance aside, the reduction and near elimination of flare in many situations is, in itself, worth the extra few bucks you might have to pay for a coated lens. Should you shoot any color film, coated optics will provide far better results than early uncoated designs.

Number of Lens Elements. Curious about how many elements make up a given lens? If the technical specifications of the lens are unavailable, there is a simple method you can use to find out how many elements are in the lens. Hold the lens under a bright light source, and count the number of reflections in the lens. Each reflection represents one lens element. This method is not foolproof, but usually is accurate. You may need to move the lens around a bit to see all the reflections, but in doing so, be sure you don't double count. In general, it's easiest to use a single point light source, such as a fluorescent ceiling light or similar light source that is a few feet above the lens itself and won't cast reflections that are difficult to

count. For interchangeable lenses, I also recommend putting on the rear lens cap to have a dark "background" to make the reflections clearer. With old folding cameras, TLRs, and other lenses that use leaf shutters, be sure to fire the shutter and hold it open on the "bulb" setting when counting; if you don't, all you'll get is a count for the front elements plus one reflection off the shutter blades.

To practice counting elements, pick a lens with known technical specifications and a known number of elements, and then count the reflections. When you can reliably count the number of reflections, you're set to go. What you'll find is that some lenses are incredibly easy to count, while others are a true pain. Uncoated lenses can be especially difficult, due to internal reflections. Zoom lenses are absolute headaches. Only current wide angle lenses, zooms, and a few telephoto lenses will exceed six elements, so if your count goes over six, you probably made a mistake. Older folding cameras and TLRs generally have three to five lens elements; more desirable lenses have four or more.

☐ Film Formats

Unlike 35mm cameras, where the negative size has been standardized to 24mm x 36mm, medium format cameras cover a wide range of aspect ratios and negative sizes—from rectangular, to the unique 6cm x 6cm square format. This wide selection of formats allows for greater creative freedom and gives photographers the ability to choose the formats that best match their styles and needs.

In looking at medium format cameras, realize that there is no "best" format. Each format has its strengths and weaknesses, and selecting the correct format depends more on your own preferences and shooting style than any other factor.

"...medium format cameras cover a wide range of aspect ratios and negative sizes."

645. The 645 format (taking its name from its size—roughly 6cm x 4.5cm) represents the smallest physical film format in medium format today, but also represents one of the most versatile. Since Mamiya introduced their 645 camera in 1975, and Bronica introduced the Bronica ETR in 1976,

□ Aspect Ratios

As you can see from the charts on page 8, the aspect ratio of both the negative and print can vary. In general, prints 8"x10" and larger have been "standardized" to a 1:1.25 aspect ratio. This should be kept in mind if you have all your printing done by a professional lab. However, if the 1:1.25 ratio does not fit the photograph, you can vary the size of the print to match the size and aspect ratio you're looking for. As a predominantly 645 shooter, I find that when I use a professional lab much of my work prints best on 11"x14", as the aspect ratio of the print is closest to that of the negative. In my own darkroom, prints vary greatly in size and aspect ratio. Choose the film format which best fits your own preferences, and remember that professional labs can crop to your desired composition.

One of the key advantages to medium format photography is increased creative control; you are not subject to the same restrictions on print sizes and cropping often seen with 35mm negatives. Labs are much more responsive to the needs of their medium format customers, since many medium format photographers are professionals depending on their photographs for income. Most labs consider medium format printing "custom" work, and thus won't charge extra for cropping, dodging, burning, or odd print sizes. Just include a note to leave a border if necessary when requesting an odd-sized print, since most labs print odd-sized prints on the closest-size standard paper.

the 645 format has gained a great deal of popularity, especially with wedding photographers and those photographing in the field. In general, 645 equipment is smaller and lighter than equivalent cameras in larger formats, while also offering a wider range of features. Looking at the modern 645 cameras, many of them represent the easiest transition from 35mm cameras, with grips, automation, and handling reminiscent of an oversized 35mm SLR. It should also be noted that the only medium format cameras currently featuring autofocus are in the 645 format.

The actual size of a 645 negative is 41.5mm x 56mm, 2.7 times that of a standard 35mm negative with an aspect ratio of 1:1.35. The 645 format offers the most exposures per standard roll of all medium format cameras—fifteen to sixteen exposures, depending on the camera. This makes the format the

most economical of all medium format cameras on a cost-per-frame basis.

Being the smallest of the medium formats, some people think that it achieves slightly less quality than 6x6 and the larger formats, but this is truly not the case. When making an 8"x10" print from a 6x6 negative, the negative is cropped down to nearly the same dimensions as a 645 negative. As a result, prints from 6x6 and 645 are virtually identical in sharpness and apparent grain. It should also be noted that all medium format negatives represent a tremendous increase in quality over 35mm negatives, and 645 is no exception. The difference in quality between prints made from a 645 negative and prints from a 6x6 (or larger) negative will not be very significant in print sizes under 16"x20".

□ Note

It should be noted that not all 645 cameras have exactly the same format size. Some, such as the Bronica ETR series cameras, have a slightly larger 42.5mm x 56mm negative, and a 1:1.31 aspect ratio.

Those insisting on the absolute best medium format can offer may wish to look into 6x7 or larger formats, but for most people stepping into medium format, 645 offers a solid option—particularly for those seeking autofocus, autoexposure, and other more "advanced" features. The only downside is that most 645 equipment is available only in modern SLR and rangefinder cameras. Because of this, there is a limited quantity of inexpensive folding cameras and other, older, used equipment available on the market.

6x6. 6x6 is by far the most popular size in medium format, and it comes as no surprise that 6x6 has the greatest variety of available equipment. From old rangefinders, to the classic Rollei TLR cameras and legendary Hasselblad SLRs, 6x6 is synonymous with medium format. Perhaps the greatest advantage of the format is the ability to crop. When taking a photo, the composition is square, which eliminates the need for vertical or horizontal framing. Instead, cropping can be done easily in the darkroom. This also makes handling 6x6 cameras easier, because you need not turn the camera for a vertical shot. Again, simply take the photograph and then crop to a vertical composition in the darkroom.

As a result of this ease in shooting, many people feel that photographs taken with 6x6 cameras have a more "relaxed" feel, since the photographer isn't confined to a rectangular format. However, there is a downside; since you expect to crop 6x6 negatives in the darkroom, there can be a temptation to shoot too loosely. If excessive cropping is needed to correct this in the darkroom, it decreases the quality of the final image and reduces the advantage of 6cm x 6cm over 35mm and rectangular medium formats. As long as care is taken not to shoot too loosely, though, 6x6 offers great creative freedom, as negatives can be easily cropped to any print size with excellent quality.

While most prefer 6x6 for the ability to crop, the square format itself should not be overlooked. Too many photographers use 6x6 cameras and simply crop down to fit 8"x10" or other standard print sizes. As the photo below shows, square images are both unique and quite effective.

Like 645 equipment, 6x6 cameras are relatively compact and very easy to use in the field. Many pho-

tographers enjoy the ability to obtain high quality results both in the studio and out in the field, making 6x6 SLR cameras a favorite with both professionals and amateurs. There is also a plethora of excellent new and used 6x6 cameras on the market in every category, making 6cm x 6cm an excellent choice.

6x7. For those demanding the highest quality possible out of their medium format negatives, 6x7 offers the best option. Because the negative size is significantly larger than either a 645 or 6x6 negative, and requires minimal cropping for most standard print sizes, images from a 6x7 provide noticeably higher quality.

The downside is that 6x7 equipment tends to be larger, heavier, and less portable than other medium format cameras. The Mamiya RB and RZ-67, for example, have reputations as the best medium format studio cameras, but only a few hearty souls take these beasts into the field. Only the Pentax 6x7 seems to have a solid following among landscape photographers, yet those photographers rarely carry more than two lenses. Even then, the heavy mirror slap of 6x7 cameras demands the use of a tripod and mirror lockup to prevent loss of sharpness due to vibrations. Only the 6x7 rangefinder cameras offer the advantage of 6x7 negatives with good portability. However, most rangefinder cameras offer very limited lens selection, and problems with parallax and filter use also become an issue.

If you need the best that medium format can offer and don't mind the limitations, 6x7 is the best option.

6x8. Found only in a few cameras, the 6x8 format is an unconventional negative size offering slightly higher quality than

Camera: Rolleicord V

6x7. In most respects, 6x8 equipment shares the problems of 6x7 in terms of size, weight, and portability. However, the difference in image quality between the two formats is largely negligible, and choosing between the two should be made on the basis of the cameras and your specific needs.

6x9. Offering the largest negatives in medium format, the 6x9 negative also gives virtually the same aspect ratio seen in standard 35mm negatives. However, given the fact that exact negative size can vary from 56mm x 82mm to 56mm x 88mm, the term 6x9 may be a bit inaccurate. In any case, the 6x9 format is unique from the other formats in two very important regards.

First, there are no 6x9 SLR cameras currently on the market. If there were, the size and weight of the equipment would likely render it extremely unpopular. As it is, the Fuji rangefinder cameras in 6x9, favorites in this format for field use, are not the smallest of cameras. Other popular 6x9 field cameras, such as the Linhof Master Technika 6x9, are only slightly smaller and lighter than 4x5 cameras.

Second, 6x9 is a popular format with large format photographers. Field and view cameras, such as the Linhof Super Technika 23 or Arca-Swiss M-line 6cm x 9cm, dominate the 6x9 camera market, and are extremely popular as alternatives to 4x5 cameras due to the lower cost of 120 film and processing and more compact size of 6x9 equipment compared to 4x5. This makes 6x9 extremely popular with architectural photographers and those who need extensive camera movements without getting into a 4x5 rig. The 6x9 format also works extremely well for fans of ultrawide photography, because lenses (such as the Schneider 47mm Super Angulon or the Rodenstock Grandagon lenses) with focal lengths down to 35mm are available and provide extreme wide-angle views on 6x9 film.

As a result, 6x9 is recommended to those who need extensive camera movements, those who want the added size or wide-angle capability of the 6x9 negative, and photographers who prefer the 1:1.5 aspect ratio found in the standard 35mm negative.

◻ Film Processing and Costs

Film Cost. Does it cost a lot more to shoot in medium format? Not really. The major expense in medium format is the camera equipment, not the film and development, as many people think. If you buy an

◻ Exposures per Roll of Film

FORMAT	EXPOSURES PER ROLL
35mm	12/24/36
645	15-16
6x6	12
6x7	10
6x8	9
6x9	8
4x5	1 per sheet

Note: Exposures for medium format are based on 120 film. Cameras able to use 220 film will achieve twice the number of exposures when using 220 film. 4x5 film comes in sheets, not rolls, with one exposure per sheet. Most 4x5 film holders carry two sheets.

inexpensive TLR or an older rangefinder, such as a Koni-Omega Rapid M, your cost for equipment can be equal to, or significantly lower than, an equivalent 35mm SLR system. In most cases, a roll of 120 film costs less than a 24 or 36 exposure roll for 35mm. In some cases, 120 film costs approximately half of its 35mm counterpart—particularly in professional slide films. This means that while your cost-per-shot in medium format is higher than in 35mm, the difference isn't quite as hefty as you might think.

Developing Cost. As for developing costs, 120 processing can be the same or cheaper than 35mm. At most labs, the price for development of 120 film is the same as 35mm, as is the cost for prints at the time of development. As a result, developing and printing a roll of 120 film can actually cost less than 35mm, since the major expense in developing (the number of prints) is reduced. If you shoot 6x6, expect your development costs to be about the same as a twelve-exposure roll of 35mm film. For slides, developing a roll of 120 film is usually the same price as a roll of 35mm film.

The only item to watch out for is the size of the prints. With 6x6, some labs will not give you square proofs or enlargements, cropping down to a rectangular format instead. 645 and 6x7 negatives usually cause no problems, though 6x9 and larger must be handled by custom labs in most cases.

Film Consumption. When calculating the cost of medium format vs. 35mm, you also need to keep in mind that medium format photographers tend to take less photos than 35mm photographers. In

☐ Enlarging Factor: Negative Area Comparison

The chart below shows how many times a negative must be enlarged to get a certain print size.

NEGATIVE SIZE

PRINT SIZE	35mm	645	6x6	6x7	6x8	6x9	4x5
3.5"x5"	13.7	5.1	5.1	3.4	2.7	2.5	—
5"x7"	28	10	10	6.6	5.1	5.1	2
8"x10"	71.5	24	20.6	13.5	13.1	13.1	4.5
8"x12"	71.5	29.5	29.5	19.5	15.3	13.2	6.6
11"x11"	135	45	25	25	25	25	8.6
11"x14"	134	45	40.5	26.75	24.75	24.75	8.8
16"x20"	286	96	82	54	52.5	52.5	18.2

These are the numbers that really tell the tale. If you take advantage of the full negative when printing, these are the enlarging factors you should expect. As a reference, most observers consider an enlarging factor in the neighborhood of 10–15 to be "grainless" when using 100 or 400 speed film. This means that the optimal print size for 35mm is 3.5"x5", whereas an 8"x10" is optimal for 6cm x 7cm.

As you can see, there are four groups: 35mm; 645/6x6 ; 6x7/6x8/6x9, and 4x5. Results within each group will be similar on a given print size, but the larger negatives will allow for greater cropping. Each group also has noticeably better quality than the previous group, but the difference between the 645 group and the 6x7 group will not be particularly significant until the print size reaches 11"x14" or larger.

This chart also shows you the exceptional quality medium and large format can offer—prints up to 11"x14" exhibit little to no grain. You can also see just how close medium format comes to the 4x5 negative format when making 8"x10" and 11"x14" prints. Since the vast majority of people who enlarge their photos choose one of those two sizes, those are the most important numbers to look at. However, the 16"x20" figures should also be noted.

In terms of actual level of grain in the final print, a 16"x20" from medium format will be roughly equivalent to the level of grain in an 8"x10" print from 35mm, but the apparent grain to the viewer will be much less. Seem a bit counterintuitive? At first glance, it seems a preposterous notion, until you take the comfortable viewing distance into consideration. With an 8"x10" photograph, people are likely to view it from only two to three feet away, and thus will tend to notice the grain a bit more. With a 16"x20" photograph, people will view it from a greater distance, perhaps five to seven feet (or more!). The farther away from the photograph you go, the less apparent the grain appears, giving the impression of greater detail. Because the level of grain is reasonable and viewing distance is increased, a 16" x 20" print taken from a fine-grained medium format negative can often appear to rival one from 4x5 negative even when, in absolute terms, the print from 4x5 is superior.

Note that the figures provided above are close approximations for full frame printing with no borders on the final print. The table is adjusted for any necessary cropping to the negative to fit the format size (i.e., a 35mm negative is cropped to 24mm x 30mm to match the 1:1.25 aspect ratio of an 8"x10" print). It should also be noted that the closer the aspect ratio of the print to the aspect ratio of the negative, the better the results, as seen in the nonstandard 8"x11" and 11"x11" print sizes.

35mm, because film is a bit cheaper, there is a tendency to shoot more frames. In medium format, there are less shots per roll of film and photographers tend to be more careful about what they photograph. They use less film as a result. In the end, if you compare an average 35mm shooter to an average medium format shooter, you will likely find that their film and development costs are roughly the same.

Professional vs. Consumer-Grade Films. As a final note, shooting in medium format can have some added bonuses. In 35mm, the majority of photographers use standard consumer-grade films for their photos. Because of the heavy use by professionals and serious amateurs, available medium format films tend to be professional stock, not consumer grade. This means that for the same price (and often less as discussed above) as shooting a roll of standard consumer grade 35mm, you are using better quality professional grade film in your medium format camera. The result? Your photos will look a bit nicer at no added cost.

So if you are worried that moving to medium format will significantly increase your developing costs, you need not be as concerned. Depending on the type of shooting you do and your volume, you may see a moderate increase in film and processing costs or, quite possibly, a noticeable reduction if you are a low volume shooter. Many photographers also feel that, even if there is a moderate increase in cost, the quality afforded by medium format more than makes up for it.

☐ Conclusion

The mystique surrounding medium comes primarily from lack of knowledge and definitions which don't directly answer people's questions. Medium format clearly offers a high-quality alternative to 35mm photography without the difficulties involved with large format. While it must be admitted that medium format is a compromise between 35mm and large format, this compromise truly offers the best of both worlds.

"The result? Your photos will look a bit nicer at no added cost."

Fully suitable for professional photography, medium format also lends itself extremely well to everyday snapshots for the family photo album. For those looking to enter into more serious photography, or amateurs simply wanting better images at a reasonable cost, medium format is an excellent choice.

☐ Enlarging Factor—Traditional Methods vs. Negative/Print Area Comparison

Traditional methods for calculating enlarging factor take the vertical height of the print, and divide it by the vertical height of the negative. Thus, an 11"x14" print is an 11.6x enlargement from a 35mm negative (280mm ÷ 24mm), and a 6.75x enlargement from a 645 negative (280mm ÷ 41.5mm). While this presents a good look at the difference between various formats, it doesn't give as clear an indication as to why medium format is better than 35mm.

By taking into account only the vertical component, the standard method is unable to truly show the exponential advantage found by using larger negative sizes. In an 8"x10" enlargement, the difference between an 8.5x enlargement from a 35mm negative and a 5x enlargement from a 645 negative doesn't seem that great—the difference is only 3.5x. However, when you take the full area of the negative into account compared to the area of the print, that "small" 3.5x difference actually translates into a significant difference—71.5x enlargement from the 35mm negative compared to a 24x enlargement from the 645 negative. Also, at 8"x10", the difference between a 4.5x enlargement from 6x6 and a 3.7x enlargement from 6x7 doesn't seem very large, yet taking the full negative into account shows a 20.6x enlargement with the 6x6, versus a 13.5x enlargement with the 6x7. By the standard method, there is only a 22% difference between the 6x6 and 6x7, but when you take the full negative size into consideration the actual difference is 53%. As for the 35mm versus 645, the standard method reveals a mere 70% difference, while the negative area comparison shows a more accurate 298% difference between the formats in an 8"x10" print.

Thus, while this method does break with tradition, and the numbers may seem exaggerated at first glance, it does a far better job of revealing the true differences between formats.

NEGATIVE SIZE

PRINT SIZE	35mm	645	6x6	6x7	6x9	4x5
5"x7"	5.3	3.1	3.1	2.6	2.3	1.5
8"x10"	8.5	4.9	4.5	3.7	3.6	2.1
11"x14"	11.6	6.75	6.4	5.2	5.0	3.0
16"x20"	16.9	9.8	9.1	7.4	7.25	4.3

Chapter 2

Accessories and Necessities

While a good camera will provide 90% of what you need to create an excellent image, camera accessories fill that extra void and help improve results. From tripods to filters to a good light meter, having the proper accessory can make or break a photograph. In medium format photography, items such as a hand-held meter or solid tripod take on greater importance than with 35mm. Choosing the right accessories can be a challenge, yet most of the items used in 35mm carry over to medium format—cable releases, lens hoods, and other accessories are invaluable no matter what format you shoot. However, when using medium format equipment, closer attention must be paid to certain accessories to ensure they will do the job.

This chapter covers the areas of accessories often overlooked in medium format. Specifically, proper camera support and light metering are two areas photographers entering medium format often fail to consider fully. Having been pampered by built-in meters and niceties such as autoexposure, most photographers moving up from 35mm are not used to using a hand-held meter or proper metering technique. Also, too many photographers try to use improper camera support with their new medium format cameras, often resulting in lower image quality, and sometimes even resulting in broken equipment. By taking a closer look at these issues, this section explains exactly what accessories are proper for medium format use, and how to use them to best effect.

☐ Lens Care and Cleaning

Most photographers already have the majority of general accessories—lens cleaners, brushes, cable releases, and the like. However, not many photographers remember to use these accessories as needed.

Lens Cleaning. Lens cleaning, for example, is one area where the vast majority of photographers consistently come up short, yet is one of the most important areas to remember. When you get a fingerprint on your lens, clean it off immediately. Oils left by fingers are among the most damaging to lens coatings, and can easily leave permanent damage if left on the lens. Use a proper lens tissue and cleaner to remove dirt and fingerprints, and remember to first use canned air or a brush to take off large particles and prevent scratching while cleaning. Do not use rubbing alcohol to clean your lenses as this, too, can cause serious damage to lens coatings. Cleaning and proper care of your equipment will ensure years of service and reduce the likelihood of repairs; lack of a regular cleaning is a primary reason why some used equipment is in such rough shape.

> "...camera accessories fill that extra void and help improve results."

Lens Hoods. Lens hoods are another item which everybody knows about, but too few photographers remember to use. Even when the sun is not causing potential for flare, a lens hood will block extraneous light from entering the lens and causing flare or ghosting. Keep the lens hood on at all times, and make sure to get hoods for all new lenses you buy.

Lens Caps. Similarly, make sure each lens has a lens cap to prevent damage—don't rely on UV filters, as a scratch on the filter is as detrimental as a scratch on the lens itself.

I cannot stress this enough—use the general accessories you already own, or make sure to add them to your camera bag on your next trip through the local photo shop.

☐ Tripods

Tripods provide camera support for situations where the shutter speed is too slow to allow for a hand-held shot. Unfortunately, proper camera support is also an often neglected area of photography. Many photographers recognize the need for a tripod in low light situations, but buy the cheapest tripod available. The reason for this is simple—most photographers only use tripods occasionally, so it seems somewhat ridiculous to spend a lot of money on an accessory that is seldom used. I agree that spending over $500 on a top-quality, carbon fiber Gitzo is not advisable for the majority of photographers, but neither is buying a cheap no-name tripod for $30.

The problem with cheap tripods is that they are usually made to handle lightweight 35mm cameras, not medium format cameras or even heavier professional 35mm cameras. Given that most medium format cameras are heavier than their 35mm counterparts, a proper tripod becomes much more important. A 35mm SLR with lens may weigh only one or two pounds, but a medium format SLR body alone can weigh that much. Add a lens and prism, and a medium format camera can exceed the maximum weight limit of most inexpensive tripods. Even with TLRs and other lighter medium format cameras, cheap tripods aren't a good idea. Inexpensive tripods are usually made primarily of plastic, and don't have the rigidity or resistance to vibration of a metal or carbon fiber tripod. Just as the mirror slap of an SLR can reduce sharpness in the negative, so can any vibrations picked up by your tripod. Another problem of cheap plastic tripods is the plastic itself. Over time, many plastics become brittle. As a result, they cannot handle as much weight, and are more prone to breaking. Even for occasional use, cheap tripods should be avoided, especially with medium format cameras.

Does this mean you need to spend a fortune to get a decent tripod? Absolutely not. When looking for a tripod, try to avoid ones made entirely of plastic—particularly those with very thin legs. A tripod with metal legs will very likely be able to carry more weight and offer greater stability. One of the best methods to test a tripod is to mount a heavy camera on it and see how stable it is at a normal working height. Hold onto the camera and apply slight downward pressure, and see how much the legs of the tripod shake or wobble. If the tripod doesn't seem stable, or the legs look like they might be starting to bow outward, move on to another model. Expect to

☐ Tripod Terminology

When looking at tripods, you'll see a variety of different features, and it can be a bit of a pain to sort it all out. Here, in no particular order, is a glossary of terms for tripods:

Load Capacity. This is the maximum amount of weight the tripod can handle before you run the risk of the tripod breaking. For tripods that have separate heads, be aware of the load capacity of the head as well as the tripod, and remember that the weight of the head counts against the maximum capacity of the tripod. For example, if you are using a three pound head on a tripod with a maximum load capacity of ten pounds, you can only put seven additional pounds of camera equipment on the tripod before you run the risk of breaking it.

Minimum Height. This refers to the lowest height of the tripod with the camera attached.

Maximum Height. This refers to the highest position the tripod can be extended. In general, shooting with a tripod at maximum height is not recommended, as it is less stable than when used at a lower height. However, you can get around this if you place sandbags on the tripod base for additional weight. Hanging sandbags on the tripod has long been a trick to increase stability and vibration resistance of tripods—the added weight helps keep the tripod in place.

Legs. Each of the three poles supporting the tripod is referred to as a leg. Depending on the tripod, legs will either extend out to one set angle, or can be set at a number of different angles. If the legs can be set at different angles, you will be able to get the camera closer to the ground—down to ten inches or less with some tripods. This is a useful feature for macro work, and also on severely uneven terrain such as in the mountains where you can extend one leg at an odd angle to get better support.

Sections. This is the number of sections each tripod leg *(continued)*

has. In most cases, tripods have three sections, which means you have two levers on each leg that are used to adjust height. To maintain stability, use as little extension of the legs as possible and extend the thicker upper sections first and the lower sections second.

Center Column. This is the center pole on which the tripod head and camera are attached. You can find either smooth center columns that are adjusted and tightened by a screw or knob at the base of the tripod, or geared center columns that adjust by a crank. In general, smooth center columns are faster to set, but geared columns give you much more precision and control. If you do copy work, macro photography, or any other work which requires precise control over camera position, a geared head is better. For general photography, a smooth center column is better (and faster). In any case, when using a tripod, adjust the height with the legs first, and raise the center column only if needed. The lower the center column, the greater the stability.

Reversible Center Columns. With certain tripods, you can reverse the center column so that the head (and camera) are attached below the tripod base. While this might seem a bit crazy, it allows you to place your camera closer to the ground, often to the point where the camera is only one inch (or less) off the ground. This can be an advantage for macro photography, or in landscapes where you want to emphasize height.

Head. This is the actual part of the tripod to which you attach the camera. On better tripods, the head can be taken off and a different head installed. For most tripods costing less than $100, the head will not be inter-

changeable and you will likely get a 3-D pan head.

2-D Pan-Tilt Head. These heads give you 360° panning, and the ability to tilt the camera up or down. No other movements are possible.

3-D Pan-Tilt Head. This is the de facto standard head for photography. You get 360° panning, the ability to tilt the camera up or down, and also tilt the camera vertically.

Geared Heads. This type of head is expensive and not the easiest to find. Geared heads give you the most precise control over camera movement.

Ball Heads. These are very popular because they allow a wide range of movements by adjusting only one screw, but you need to be careful when using ball heads with medium format cameras. Many small ball heads simply cannot handle the weight of a medium format camera. Two pound maximum load capacities are not uncommon for many of the small ball heads—about the same weight as many TLR cameras, and less than the weight of medium format SLRs and larger rangefinders. For medium format cameras, make sure to buy at least a medium ball head, and be aware that the best ball heads (with tension control) can cost over $150.

Quick Release. Instead of mounting the camera directly to the head, you mount it on a plate on the camera. This plate can then be snapped onto and removed from the camera by pushing a button or lever on the head. This makes mounting and dismounting the camera much easier than screwing the camera into the tripod. For anyone doing a great deal of tripod work, having a quick-release system and a quick-release

plate always mounted on the camera makes life much easier. Even if you don't leave the plate mounted on the camera all the time, quick-release plates are often easier to put on the camera than trying to mount the camera on a tripod with the traditional screw. Many tripods now come standard with quick-release systems, and quick-release systems can be purchased relatively inexpensively for those tripods without them. This is one of the few must-have items with tripods (other than legs and some sort of head).

"Video" Tripods. These tripods have heads with larger mounting plates for video cameras. While listed for use with video cameras, the larger plate on the head can actually provide better support for medium format cameras, which usually have larger bases the than 35mm cameras for which most less expensive tripods and heads are designed. Video tripods also have better load capacities, since video cameras tend to outweigh 35mm cameras and more closely match the weight of medium format cameras. The main disadvantage is that the head is often only a 2-D pan-tilt, which means you can only take horizontal shots unless you find some sort of L-shaped adaptor.

Bubble Levels. Sometimes a feature of the tripod, and sometimes a feature of a particular head, these little beauties (also called spirit levels) help you level the camera and tripod. This can be particularly useful on uneven ground, or when you need to make sure the tripod is level. If your tripod does not have a spirit level of some sort, head to your local hardware store. You should be able to find one that you can glue or tape to the base of your tripod (or head).

pay somewhere in the range of $60–100 for a good basic tripod, and in the neighborhood of $125–300 for a Gitzo, Bogen-Manfrotto, or similar professional tripod that will last a lifetime.

For light amateur use, a tripod in the $60–100 range will likely do the job without breaking the bank. In the lower end of this range, you'll get something with a bit more plastic and a bit less rigidity than a metal tripod, but still adequate for medium format use. In the upper range of this category, you'll find tripods made primarily of metal from makers such as Slik and Velbon. When shopping for tripods, pay careful attention to the maximum load the tripod can take. Consider a load capacity of six pounds a bare minimum for a tripod, and if you plan to use a modern medium format SLR, use an eight pounds capacity as your minimum. In general, you want to make sure the load capacity of your tripod is at least twice that of your heaviest camera to ensure stability. A tripod that will carry ten pounds would be ideal for medium format.

If you plan to use your tripod regularly, or work with heavier medium format SLR cameras, investing in a Bogen-Manfrotto, Gitzo, or similar high-end tripod is well worth the added expense. Aside from higher load capacity and better quality construction, you gain access to a wide range of accessories. Most tripods in this range do not come packaged with heads, which allows you to choose from a variety of different styles of heads. Bogen-Manfrotto, for example, offers over fifteen different tripod heads, including 3-D pan heads, ball heads, and even geared heads. And if you don't like what Bogen-Manfrotto has to offer, you can buy heads manufactured by Linhof, Kaiser, Arca-Swiss, or a number of other top manufacturers. If you consider yourself a serious amateur, professional, or would like to invest in a tripod that will truly last a lifetime, you should be looking at tripods somewhere in this price range.

As a final note, be sure to consider where the tripod will be used when making your purchase. In general, the greater the load capacity and the higher the maximum extension, the heavier the tripod is. Tripods designed for studio use can weigh as much as 26 pounds and handle the heaviest 8"x10" view cameras. This is certainly not useful to take into the field, but will provide much better support than a lighter tripod could ever provide, making it ideal for

product photography and portraiture with the camera set in a fixed position. In general, when setting up a studio, get the heaviest tripod possible. If you need to move the camera position often in your studio work, invest in a dolly or a slightly lighter tripod, but try not to get anything under eight pounds (with the head) to ensure stability. For field use, try to keep the weight of tripod and head under eight pounds. I personally find that my Bogen 3221 with head is the heaviest tripod that is still comfortable to lug around for a few hours—although I certainly prefer to have something lighter when backpacking or on long hikes. For those demanding both light weight and high load capacities, Gitzo and a few other manufacturers offer carbon fiber tripods. These are ideal for backpacking due to their exceptionally light weight and high load capacities, but often come at a hefty price. Find a tripod that best matches your needs and has all the features you require.

"These are ideal for backpacking due to their exceptionally light weight..."

Tripods to Consider. The tripods listed below offer solid quality and excellent value at their price. You will also note that the listings are tilted in favor of Bogen-Manfrotto. This is largely due to the fact that their tripods are perhaps the best known of all brands, and therefore the easiest to find and examine. Use this section as a guide as to what to look for in a tripod, not an absolute recommendation of what to buy (although you certainly won't go wrong if you purchase any of the tripods listed). There are a number of excellent tripods I have not had the opportunity to see or use, such the professional models from Cullman. Keep an eye out for products available from companies such as Majestic, Linhof, Velbon, and Gitzo, as they are well worth considering.

For a good benchmark of what a good tripod should be, take a look at the Bogen-Manfrotto 3021 (3221 for the black painted model). This tripod has a very loyal following among photographers, and for good reason. It is solid, can support any camera up to 4x5 (and even some 8x10 cameras), and take one heck of a beating and still work perfectly. At 5.75 pounds (without the head) and with a list price over

$150, the 3021 is neither the cheapest nor the lightest tripod on the market, but it will give you an idea of what to expect from the best.

In the $100 range, the Slik 300DX and Bogen 3001 are my benchmarks, with an honorable mention to the Bogen Junior Tripod #390. These tripods are lighter and a bit more limited than their more expensive brethren, but will easily support medium format cameras. For those on a budget, tripods like these are ideal as they have both the load capacity and high quality, while only sacrificing a few features found in pricier models (mainly maximum height and some load capacity).

☐ Filters

Filters can make one of the most useful additions to a photographer's arsenal. For both corrective purposes and dramatic effects, filters can often provide the edge that makes or breaks a photograph. One of the best sources on filters is free from most dealers—the product catalog from any major filter manufacturer. Sales brochures are often overlooked due to the fact that they are designed by the manufacturer to make you buy their product. In the case of filters, however, the information these brochures and catalogs provide is superior to what is found in most books on general technique. Not only do the catalogs list available products, they almost always include photographs showing the effect of the filter and the recommended uses. However, for information on filters for a specific area of photography, find a good book on the subject in question.

Polarizers. Of all filters, a polarizer is undoubtedly one of the most useful to have. It will darken skies, intensify colors, and remove unwanted reflections. Additionally, polarizers are manufactured on rotating mounts, thus allowing for the filter's effect to be continuously varied. The only source of confusion in polarizers is a "circular" polarizer vs. a standard "linear" polarizer. Both have the same effect, but a circular polarizer often costs nearly twice as much. The reason is that a circular polarizer is corrected so that it will not interfere with autofocus systems or TTL metering systems that meter using the SLR's mirror. In general, medium format cameras can use standard linear polarizers, since there usually isn't a TTL or autofocus system to contend with. However, for those using the latest cameras with autofocus or TTL

metering, check your camera's manual to see which filter type you should use.

UV Filters. One of the greatest debates in photography has been over UV and skylight filters, often sold by camera salesmen to "protect" the expensive lens you just purchased. Many have posed the question, is that darn piece of clear glass really worth spending money on? Depending on who you talk to, the answer can be an emphatic *yes* or a resounding *no*. To make matters more difficult, neither the naysayers nor the UV supporters tend to have their facts straight.

Photographic purists are quick to point out that filters, even the "clear" UV filters, have some effect on the final image. Additionally, by putting a filter on the lens, you are putting another piece of glass between your subject and the negative, which can degrade image quality. Finally, purists point out that if camera manufacturers felt a UV filter was a necessary accessory for a lens, they would have either included one with the lens or recommended buying one in their product literature. Instead, manufacturers include only a lens cap to protect the lens, and neither include nor recommend a UV filter to protect the lens. While the first two arguments have merit, the third is more myth than fact.

In truth, any filter you put in front of the lens will have an effect on the negative. If you look at something through a UV filter and then look at the same subject without the UV filter, you will notice a difference. Making the same comparison with a skylight filter will result in more pronounced results as skylight filters have a light red tint and a stronger effect. However, UV and skylight filters also help in cutting haze, which can actually improve the final image. In the end, the purists are correct—these filters will affect the final image, for better or worse, and you need to be aware of this.

> "...any filter you put in front of the lens will have an effect on the negative."

Purists are also correct to point out that any additional piece of glass between the subject and the negative can have a detrimental effect on the final image. But the key here is *can*, not *will*. Much of this question rests on the quality of filter you buy more than any other factor. Cheap, no-name filters are far more likely to cause problems than name-brand filters from companies such as Hoya, Tiffen, B+W, or Heliopan. The reason for this is simple; the cheap brands often don't use quality glass, don't make sure each filter is of uniform thickness, mount their filters in cheap plastic rings (which are more prone to misalignment) and, most importantly, don't offer any sort of coating. Each of these factors is a recipe for disaster, and can result in flare or other optical aberrations that will degrade the final image. Better quality filters from known brands use optical quality glass, brass rings which provide better alignment and longevity, and often have some sort of coating on them (multicoating is best, but often costs extra). The best filters from B+W and Heliopan are made using only the highest quality Schott glass, and are produced under strict quality control to ensure uniform thickness and clarity. As a result, filters from known quality brands reduce the possibility of image degradation to almost nothing. However, it should be noted that the purists are correct—any filter in front of the lens can affect the final image, and using even the highest quality filter increases the likelihood of flare and other problems.

The third argument often touted by purists is that if the lens maker thought a UV filter was necessary, they would have included it with the lens. Unfortunately, this argument is more myth than fact. UV filters, like any filter, are optional accessories, and thus, manufacturers do not include them. It should be noted that, while filters are not included, nearly every lens has a threaded ring or other method to mount filters. Simply because the lens maker does not include a UV filter with a new lens means nothing, and this argument should be ignored.

"...protect the value of your lenses by keeping the optics in top condition."

My favorite argument against filters, and the biggest myth of them all, is the cost issue. Some people have suggested that the filters you buy cost the store only $1 or $2, and when the salesman sells it to you for $20 the motivation is huge profit, not actual usefulness for the customer. Having worked in a camera store and seen the dealer cost for filters, I can assure you this argument is completely bogus; camera stores pay significantly more than $1 or $2 for each filter. While filters do carry a larger markup than most other items, the profit is nowhere near as large as is suggested by the myth. Of all myths about filters, this is the first you should ignore.

Those recommending UV filters tend to have slightly better arguments, but still include quite a bit of misinformation. Many suggest that any UV filter will do the job, and thus, you can get away with a cheap filter or a used one. However, as mentioned earlier, cheap filters can be accidents waiting to happen, and are not recommended. Used filters are a mixed bag; if you decide to buy one, inspect the glass and mount for any imperfections. If there are any dents in the mount or scratches on the glass, don't buy it. I have also found that the vast majority of used filters are inexpensive ones, and rarely does a Heliopan or B+W filter find its way into the used section. Supporters also tend to downplay the effect of UV filters on the final image, but as purists point out, a filter will have a noticeable effect on the final image and can increase the chances for flare and other problems.

Perhaps the strongest argument for using a UV filter is to protect the lens from damage. Should a lens become scratched or chipped, the cost to replace the damaged lens element can easily cost $75–150. When photographing a public speaker at Dickinson College a few years ago, I happened to catch my lens on the corner of a door latch, leaving a nasty scratch on my filter. After a moment of cursing under my breath, I threw the filter away and continued photographing the event without any further trouble. Given that most UV filters cost less than $30 (except for expensive multicoated versions), you can buy at least three to five UV filters for the same cost as having the lens repaired once. Thus, UV filters can provide cheap insurance and help protect the value of your lenses by keeping the optics in top condition. However, it must be remembered that a fingerprint or scratch on a filter can be as detrimental as a scratch or fingerprint on the lens itself. Filters need to be cleaned regularly, and should be replaced if damaged.

In the end, is a UV filter worth it? For me, the answer relies on three factors. First, is the front element of the lens prone to damage? With my Bronica's 75mm lens, the front element is recessed far enough into the lens that damage is unlikely, so I stick with the purists and don't use a UV filter with that lens. On the other hand, the front element of my 150mm lens is somewhat large and could be damaged by accidentally bumping into something, so I have a UV filter on it in case of accidental damage. Second, will I want to trade or sell the lens sometime in the future? If so, a UV filter is good insurance to help keep optics perfect and resale value intact. If I intend to keep the lens indefinitely, I default to my third deciding factor: do I want to follow the purists example, or use a UV filter and accept the effect it has on the image? In most cases, I have decided to use a UV filter, largely because I cannot afford to replace damaged lens elements. However, I have been known to remove the UV filter when shooting as insurance against flare and other potential problems. My recommendation? Buy the UV filter and consider it cheap insurance, then remove it when you want to guard against potential flare.

☐ Light Meters

One common argument against medium format cameras is that a hand-held meter is often required. Considering that sophisticated multi-segment meters are offered on current autofocus SLR cameras, and that meters have been built into most 35mm cameras produced since the 1960s, it seems strange that medium format cameras don't have built-in meters—or have them available only as a separate option. However, the answer is far simpler than one would expect: *accuracy.* Simply stated, using a hand-held meter can produce far more accurate and consistent exposures than even the latest multi-segment meter found in top 35mm SLRs. As a result, most professionals and serious amateurs use hand-held meters rather than relying on built-in meters, which can be less accurate.

Medium format manufacturers, whose main customer base has traditionally been serious amateurs and professionals, refrained from including built-in meters on their cameras for two reasons. First, they recognized that a built-in meter was an unnecessary item for a significant portion of their customers who relied on hand-held meters for more accurate results. Second, manufacturers wanted to give their systems flexibility and allow photographers to customize the camera to their personal needs. While some photog-

raphers wanted bare-bones mechanical workhorses with only waist-level finders, others demanded the same features in their medium format cameras that were found in 35mm SLRs. Thus, manufacturers made available metered prisms and other accessories as options rather than built-in features.

> ## "...using a hand-held meter can produce more accurate and consistent exposures."

In current cameras, pressure to include more advanced systems such as multi-segment meters and autofocus has resulted in a shift away from these traditional lines, and cameras such as the Pentax 645n include both built-in meters, autoexposure, and autofocus capabilities. However, the majority of medium format equipment, particularly cameras on the used market, do not include built-in meters as standard equipment. At first glance, this appears to be a disadvantage, but as outlined above, hand-held meters offer greater accuracy, and equipment manufacturers had a justifiable method to their madness of not including meters in their cameras.

Accuracy, Consistency and Exposure. In order to obtain a good negative, you need more than a camera and light meter; you must have an ACE up your sleeve. (Every book needs at least one bad pun, so here it is. I can assure you that the remainder of the book is utterly devoid of such senseless assaults on the mind.) Creating good, printable negatives requires three components: accuracy, consistency, and exposure.

Accuracy is determined by your light meter; you need to have a meter, built-in or hand-held, which will give you accurate readings. Possibly the most important and often overlooked component is consistency. Not only must your meter and camera equipment be accurate, it must be consistent and reliable. Just as a shutter that fires anywhere from $1/60$ to $1/250$ when set at $1/125$ cannot be trusted, a meter must be able to give you an accurate reading and be consistently accurate in all situations, from low light to severe backlighting. The final component, exposure, refers to the camera itself. Once you have accuracy and consistency, you need to have a camera that can reliably take your photographs. In general, a properly-maintained camera solves the exposure requirement, leaving only accuracy and consistency unanswered.

In looking at the question of accuracy, hand-held meters allow for greater exposure control and accuracy than built-in meters can offer. The reason for this lies in just how built-in meters work in comparison to a hand-held. Built-in meters take reflective measurements—they measure the amount of light reflecting off the subject (generally what you see in the viewfinder) and give an averaged reading for proper exposure. While this sounds like a reasonably accurate method, built-in meters can be fooled easily. Here's how:

Built-in meters read light reflecting off everything in the metering area, which is generally the entire image area in most SLR cameras. It then takes an overall reading, and averages it to give a proper exposure based on an 18% reflectance reading, which is the "middle gray" tone. The 18% reflectance is a de facto standard for proper exposure, and built-in meters provide readings assuming that your subject is middle gray. Unfortunately, very few subjects actually have an 18% reflectance, meaning any areas of excessive brightness or low light can throw off the reading and cause the meter to read higher or lower than intended, resulting in under- or overexposure.

In photos involving large amounts of sky, snow scenes, or large bright areas, most reflective meters will underexpose by one to two stops. This includes both hand-held reflective meters, built-in meters, and the latest multi-segment meters built into today's top autofocus cameras. Situations involving backlighting are especially difficult for hand-held meters to deal with, and I have yet to use any reflective meter or built-in meter that fully compensates in these situations. Likewise, when taking photos involving large dark areas, the vast majority of reflective meters will overexpose the negative by one to two stops. Camera manufacturers have struggled against these difficulties, and attempt to solve them with sophisticated multi-segment meters. Unfortunately, despite ingenious technology such as the color meter found in the Nikon F5, built-in meters can still be fooled.

Does this mean that built-in meters are inherently inaccurate, and the 18% reflectance standard is incorrect? Yes, and no. Built-in meters are inherently inaccurate when compared to a hand-held meter in absolute terms. In relative terms, built-in meters

work reasonably well in most situations when compared to hand-held meters. The reason for this is that film latitude allows for some inaccuracy. Color film, for example, can be under or overexposed up to two stops and still provide a good print. As built-in meters generally give readings within this range in normal situations, the improved accuracy from using hand-held meter does necessarily provide better results.

The trouble begins when shooting in difficult situations, as previously described, or when the film latitude is small enough to reveal inaccuracies of a built-in meter. In black and white photography, overexposure latitude is 1–1½ stops, but underexposure latitude is only ⅔ stop, as black and white film is somewhat tolerant of overexposure, but not very forgiving of underexposure. Color slide film, on the other hand, is very intolerant of exposure errors, and exposure differences as little as ⅓ stop can have a serious impact on the negative. Where built-in meters can work well with color film, black and white begins to reveal inaccuracies, and slide film can truly embarrass built-in meters.

Bracketing, taking the same photo numerous times, intentionally underexposing and overexposing some shots, will ensure you obtain at least one good negative, but at the cost of additional film. Hand held meters, on the other hand, can eliminate the need for bracketing due to their greater accuracy, cutting down your film expenditure.

"Built-in meters read light reflecting off everything in the metering area..."

Unlike built-in meters, which are simply variations on reflective meters, hand-held meters come in four different varieties—reflective, ambient, spot-meter, and flashmeter. Each works slightly differently, but is capable of delivering accurate and consistent exposure. Before choosing a meter, make sure you understand the strengths and weaknesses of each type of meter. Select the meter that best fits your needs and shooting style.

Reflective Meters. Reflective meters, as their name implies, measure the light reflected off the subject and give an average reading based on the 18% reflective standard. Built-in meters, as you may have

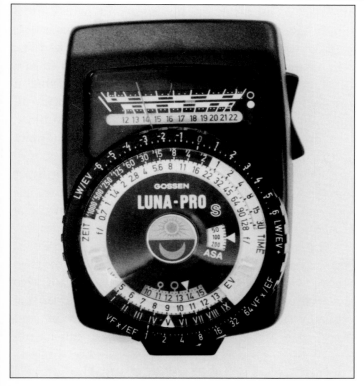 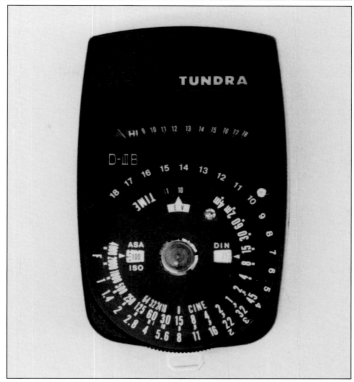

(Left) The Gossen Luna-Pro has been the "standard" hand-held meter for professional use for many years. Exceptionally accurate and very well built, the Luna-Pro is easily one of the best meters available on the market, new or used. Built for reflective readings, it also offers a sliding white dome for ambient readings, making the meter very versatile. After making a reading, the needle locks in place, making it much easier to keep track of the correct exposure. A great meter, period.

(Right) The Tundra D-IIIB is a much lower-cost meter styled after the Luna-Pro. Like the Gossen, the Tundra includes a sliding white dome for ambient readings. However, the readouts are greatly simplified, and do not provide as much information as the Luna-Pro does. Also, the needle does not lock on this model, which means you have to note the reading immediately when you take it. The accuracy of the meter is reasonable, and I have used mine with good results on black and white film. However, for more serious work or when using slide film, I have found that meters such as the Luna-Pro are more accurate. The Tundra, which can be found for under $100, is a good example of what you'll find in a low-cost hand-held meter, and is significantly smaller in size than a Luna-Pro or other professional meter.

guessed already, are in fact reflective meters. While built-in meters measure light through the taking lens, hand-held meters measure a broad angle of reflected light, usually equivalent to what a built-in meter would measure with a 35mm or 50mm lens (the instruction manual should tell you the exact angle). At first glance, it may seem as if a hand-held reflective meter is worse than one built into the camera. After all, it isn't measuring exactly what light is coming through the lens, and you can't be 100% sure of what the meter is reading. However, you will find that a hand-held reflective meter is better than many of the built-in multi-segment meters found

in the most expensive 35mm and medium format cameras.

The reason is consistency. Multi-segment meters are designed to compensate under certain conditions, such as backlighting. However, while you know the meter will compensate, the question still remains—will it compensate correctly, or still be off? If you try to second-guess a multi-segment meter, the likelihood is that you will only cause a worse exposure than what the camera calculated. In these same difficult situations, a hand-held reflective meter will undoubtedly read incorrectly, but it will consistently read incorrectly. Given some experience, you will begin to understand exactly which situations cause the hand-held meter trouble, and learn to compensate your exposures accordingly. For example, in tough backlighting situations, I know that my hand-held reflective meter consistently gives a read-

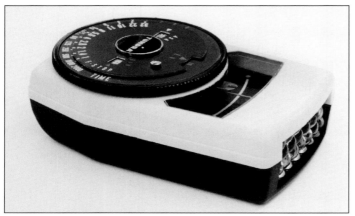

Look, Ma! No batteries! Some meters, such as this inexpensive Tundra, do not require batteries. Instead, there is a photosensitive diode in the meter that continuously reacts to light. The downside— these meters tend to be reflective meters only, and accuracy isn't quite as good as more expensive meters. Also, over time, the meter will lose accuracy as the photosensitive diode begins to die.

When metering off the gray card as shown, make sure you don't cast a shadow on the card, as that can throw off your reading. Also, make sure the card is pointing towards the camera position to make sure you are accurately measuring the light falling on the scene as your camera sees it.

ing that would result in two stops underexposure. I simply take a reading and then adjust exposure two stops to compensate for the meter's error. On the other hand, the multi-segment meter in my 35mm autofocus camera will indicate an exposure that is anywhere from dead accurate to two stops off, depending on the lens, how close I am to the subject, how much of the background is in the photograph, and a number of other factors. Trying to second-guess the meter and figure out how far off exposure may be is impossible, and I am forced to trust the meter in the camera or bracket my shots to ensure at least one usable negative.

For the highest-quality results, consistency of your equipment can be far more important than accuracy. Just as a shutter set at $^1/_{60}$ second that always fires at $^1/_{40}$ second is better than a shutter that fires anywhere from $^1/_{45}$ second to $^1/_{75}$ second (less than $^1/_{15}$ second error with the more accurate shutter

---

☐ **How to Use a Reflective Meter.**

Method One is the standard method of metering with a reflective meter. In most cases, it will give you a good reading to work with. For landscapes and other photographs taken outdoors, be careful not to tilt the meter upwards towards the sky. Keep the meter level, or point it slightly downward for best results.

Method One
1. Check to make sure the meter is in good working order and batteries are fresh.
2. Point the meter at your subject and take reading.
3. Set camera accordingly and take photograph.

Method Two allows the meter to read light striking the subject at the proper 18% reflectance off the gray card, thus giving you the best average exposure without the meter being fooled by bright or dark subjects. This method can be very accurate given a little practice, and can turn an inexpensive reflective meter into a virtual "ambient" meter.

Method Two
1. Put 18% gray card in front of subject, pointing back towards camera position.
2. Take reflective reading off the gray card, making sure to meter only the gray card. To do this, hold the meter only 6"–8" away from the gray card.
3. Set camera according to the meter reading.

vs. a consistent $\frac{1}{20}$ second error with the $\frac{1}{40}$ second shutter), a hand-held meter that is consistently off in certain situations is better than a built-in meter that is technically more accurate as you can easily compensate for consistent error but not for items with variably greater accuracy. Needless to say, after less than satisfactory results with built-in meters in a number of situations, I have become an advocate of hand-held meters due to their increased consistency.

While more consistent (and accurate) than built-in meters, hand-held reflective meters share the same flaws. Because they read the light reflected off the subject, bright reflections, such as sun reflected off a lake, will cause an incorrect reading. Likewise, large dark areas in the subject, such as a model wearing a black dress, can also cause a reflective meter to give an inaccurate reading. Backlighting and other difficult lighting situations can also cause problems, and this should be kept in mind. As mentioned earlier, you can often learn when a hand-held reflective meter will read incorrectly and to what degree, but reflective meters, both built-in and hand-held, tend to be the least accurate of all meters.

Ambient Meters. Ambient meters are extremely accurate and reliable, and are often the choice of professionals. Rather than measure the light reflecting off the subject, ambient meters measure the exact amount of light striking the subject. The difference is substantial; in cases of heavy glare, such as the sun reflecting off a lake, the ambient meter will not be fooled by the excessive amount of light reflecting off the lake. Likewise, ambient meters will not be fooled by excessively dark areas in your subject. An ambient meter will quickly and easily give you the correct exposure, and for "what you see is exactly what you get" metering, ambient meters can't be beat. Ambient meters also can be used for fast and accurate measurement of backlighting. By first taking a normal ambient reading and then turning the meter 180° for a second reading, you can quickly determine the amount of backlighting—a great boon to those shooting with fill flash.

However, ambient meters do have two important drawbacks. First, ambient meters measure the amount of light striking the subject, but sometimes you can't get right next to your subject. One good example is taking photographs in the theater. During a performance, the lights on stage are generally quite bright, while the audience sits under dimmed light-

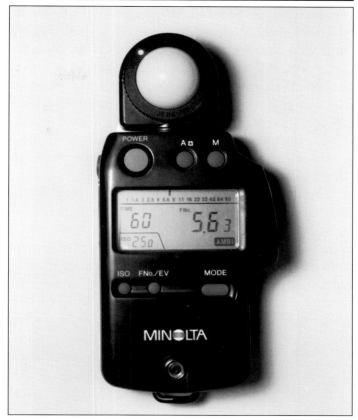

Minolta Autometer IVf, a typical modern ambient meter with LCD display. Accurate to $\frac{1}{10}$ of a stop, and with a wide range of functions, including the ability to store and average multiple readings.

Note that the meter is pointing directly back at the camera position to ensure the meter measures the light striking the subject exactly as the camera sees it. Tilting the meter in any other direction could have thrown off the reading and resulted in improper exposure.

ing, thus taking an ambient reading in the audience will result in severe overexposure. Since jumping up on stage to take a quick reading with your ambient meter would likely result in your being ejected from the theater, a reflective or spotmeter must be used. The second problem is that ambient meters will not tell you the contrast range of your subject. This can be very important if you need to control exactly how your subject is rendered on film, or want to adjust the contrast of the scene for creative effect.

Overall, ambient meters are one of the best to have available to you for general photography, as they give very accurate and consistent results in a variety of difficult situations. Many ambient meters can also be used as reflective meters or spotmeters with specific attachments, making them one of the most versatile types of meters available.

Spotmeters. Of all the types of meters, spotmeters are by far the most capable of giving you the best possible exposure. Unfortunately, they are also the most difficult to use of all meters. Essentially, a spotmeter is a reflective meter that measures a very narrow angle of view. While so-called "spot attachments" measure a 5–10° angle of view, most photographers consider a true spotmeter to be one that measures only 1°. The reason for this is simple—a 5–10° angle often cannot isolate specific tones of your subject, only small, partial areas. A 1° spotmeter, on the other hand, allows the user to meter very specific areas of the subject—essential to calculating the contrast range of your subject or setting exposure based on one important element. As a result of such precise readings, spotmeters offer the photographer greater accuracy, consistency, and control over the final image than any other type of meter.

The downside is ease of use; spotmeters require more of the photographer than standard reflective or ambient meters. While a spotmeter will read very specific areas of your subject, the readings you get from the meter are based on 18% reflectance. This means that the meter will give you a reading based on the assumption that you want the selected area to be middle gray on the negative. Thus, you can't simply meter one element of the subject and take the photo, unless that element happens to be a 18% reflectance (which is highly unlikely). In most cases, you will need to take and average multiple readings, or adjust the exposure of your first reading to get proper exposure. In either case, more thought (and math) is required than with other meters, but far greater exposure control and accuracy is possible. If you demand the most accurate results, or require complete control over every aspect of the exposure, spotmeters are the only way to go. However, it should be noted

---

☐ How to Use an Ambient Meter

1. Check your meter to make sure it is functioning properly.
2. Place the meter in front of your subject, making sure the white dome is pointing back at the camera position. Make sure you stand off to the side as shown to avoid blocking the white dome.
3. Now take the meter reading.
4. Set the shutter and aperture as indicated by the meter. Adjust the meter reading for a specific setting.

☐ Checking Meter Accuracy

As mentioned earlier, make sure the batteries in the meter are fresh and the meter is working properly. You can check your meter's accuracy using one of the three following methods:

1. The easiest and most accurate method is to head to a local camera shop that sells ambient meters and check your meter against a new one or a used meter that has been professionally checked.
2. The second method is to purchase a Kodak 18% gray card. Then use a reflective meter or a camera's built-in meter to read the amount of light reflecting off the gray card. Be careful to measure only the gray card, and not anything else! Bring the camera or reflective meter close to the card if necessary. Note the reading, and then take a reading of the gray card with your ambient meter.
3. If your ambient meter has the option of taking reflective readings, install the reflective metering attachment (or slide the dome out of the way). Then measure the light reflecting off an 18% gray card and compare it to a reflective meter or a camera's built-in meter.

As long as your meter is within $\frac{1}{3}$ stop of the reading taken with the other meter, everything is in good working order. If the readings differ more than $\frac{1}{3}$ stop, replace the battery and check again. If the readings are still significantly different, have the meter checked and recalibrated.

☐ How to Use a Spotmeter

Unlike with ambient and reflective meters, there are more than one or two methods for using a spotmeter. The first method is the simplest, and is also the way to determine the contrast range of your subject.

Method 1: Simple Averaging. To meter by the "simple averaging" method, use the spotmeter to take two separate readings, one highlight and one shadow. You then take the two readings and average them together. While it sounds simple, a little extra care needs to be taken, as outlined in these directions:

1. Meter the brightest highlight in which you want detail in the final print. Note the meter reading. Please note that simply metering a cloud because it is the brightest object in the photo will not work, and could skew your calculations towards underexposure. You need to make sure the highlight you choose is the brightest one in which you want detail in the final image.

2. Take a reading of the darkest shadow in which you want detail in the final print. Note this meter reading. Again, simply metering the darkest shadow can skew the final exposure calculation, so take care to measure the darkest shadow in which you want detail.

3. Now average the two readings. For example, if the highlight reading was $1/125$ second at f16, and the shadow reading was $1/125$ second at f4, there is four stops difference between the two readings. Take the difference and divide it by two, to get two stops. Add two stops to your shadow reading or take two stops away from your highlight reading, and you get your aver-

aged reading of $1/125$ second at f8. By exposing at $1/125$ sec at f8 (or an equivalent exposure time), you will get the correct exposure to have detail in both highlight and shadow, and everything else in the photo should fall into place.

In general, as long as your shadow and highlight readings are within seven stops of each other, you will obtain your desired results. If the difference is greater than seven stops, you run the risk of blowing out the chosen highlight and having a complete lack of detail in the chosen shadow area. This is because the contrast range exceeds the abilities of the film or the paper used to print the final image. In any case, metering the highlight and shadow as outlined above has an added bonus—the difference in stops between highlight and shadow tells you the contrast range of your subject. The greater the difference between your chosen highlight and shadow, the greater the contrast range of your subject. Likewise, if the difference is small (only two to three stops), you are dealing with a low contrast subject. This is of great help when selecting the correct film or anticipating how the negative will look when printed. With a lower contrast range, the print will be largely midtones with little extremes in contrast. Likewise, a wide contrast range of seven stops or more will result in extremes in contrast on the final print. In all, the "simple averaging" technique does a great deal not only in determining correct exposure, but also in giving you information on the contrast range of the subject.

Method 2: Averaging Multiple Readings. In some cases, using a simple averaging will not suffice, particularly if you need to ensure certain

areas of the subject are exposed correctly and have detail. For example, taking a photograph in the woods may not lend itself to simple averaging. Simple averaging would give you correct overall exposure, but not necessarily give you the detail required in the leaves, foliage, and items on the ground making up the shadows. In this case, you would need to take more readings and then adjust your exposure towards the shadow detail, depending on your desired effect. Unfortunately, outlining a method of doing this is difficult as the number of readings required and the amount you need to compensate varies greatly depending on the given situation. Instead, I suggest the following:

1. Follow the simple averaging technique. This will give you the overall contrast range of the scene, and give you a basic exposure time.

2. Take additional readings, and see how far off the average reading they are. Increase or decrease the exposure depending on whether you want to emphasize the highlights or the shadows. For example, if the shadows you want to emphasize seem to be two to three stops below the average reading, increase your exposure time 1–1½ stops. This will increase detail in the shadows without blowing out the highlights.

3. Instead of step two, there is also a "quick and dirty" method that will provide reasonable results. To emphasize the shadows, take your shadow reading and then consider your highlight reading to be five stops greater. Make an average reading based on this. To emphasize the highlights, take your highlight reading and consider your shadow reading to be *(continued)*

five stops lower. Make an average reading based on this. This method can also be used for situations where you need to work quickly—the resulting negative will be accurate, or close enough that film latitude will still give you a workable negative.

In any case, a method for averaging multiple readings is something best determined by the photographer, not an author. When taking multiple readings, develop your own system that provides the results you require, but make sure to start with the simple averaging technique. It will give you the contrast range of the subject, and also a general exposure from which you can work. If you take any more than four to five readings, you stand a good chance of confusing yourself when it comes time to calculate exposure. Don't double count identical readings; if two areas of your subject read the same, only use the exposure value once in your calculations (unless you want to make sure those areas are close to middle gray). Finally, to make calculations a bit easier, use the same shutter speed or f-stop for each reading so that the difference in stops between readings is much easier to determine.

Method 3: Selecting an 18% Gray Area. The third method is the fastest method to use a spotmeter, but by far the least accurate. Rather than take multiple readings, you simply take one reading of a part of the subject that is of 18% reflectance. Simple, straightforward, and after a great deal of practice it can be a reasonably accurate method, but for the most part, I don't recommend this method unless you are doing fast shooting and don't require the most accurate results. The problem is finding that elusive area

which is of 18% reflectance. Were the world black and white, this would be easier to do, but with color, the job becomes more arduous. You need to get used to the shade of each color that represents 18% reflectance, not just what 18% gray looks like. With practice, you can become reasonably accurate, but, even with practice, absolute accuracy is compromised to a certain degree.

Method 4: The Zone System. Of all metering methods, the Zone System is perhaps the most accurate and consistent. A large part of the reason for this is that the system is not only geared towards accurate metering technique, but also extends into development and printing. The aim is to develop your own system of exposure, developing, and printing that provides consistent, repeatable, and predictable results. In general, this means specializing your choice of film and enlarging paper to a specific few (and possibly even one film and paper), of which you learn the exact characteristics. The advantage of the system is that your final images can be much better, exactly as you intended, and easier to produce. The downside is that it often takes a long period of testing to best utilize the Zone System, and if you want to try a new film you often need to go through extensive testing to fit it into your system and obtain the same level of results.

On the metering side, the Zone System is based on the following premise: the spectrum from pure white to deepest black is broken into ten segments, as seen on a Kodak Gray Scale. Each segment is called a "Zone," and assigned a number from one to ten. Zone One is pure white, while Zone Ten is pure black, and

each Zone in between represents a difference of one stop from the previous zone. Thus, Zone Three is one stop brighter than Zone Four, and one stop darker than Zone Two. At the center of the scale is Zone Five, which is of 18% reflectance. To meter, you use a spotmeter to select a specific tone in the scene and choose which zone you want to place it in. Thus, if you want the bark of a tree to be Zone Seven, take your reading and increase exposure two stops (remember that the meter will give you a reading at Zone Five, as all meters are calibrated to the 18% reflectance standard, hence the increase of two stops to move the tree bark into the desired Zone Seven). For black and white or color print films, select a shadow value to meter and choose a highlight when working with transparency (slide) film.

By selecting individual tones and choosing which zone they should be in, you get the most control over exposure, but you need to also carry through with the system in development and printing to ensure the best results. If you demand the highest-quality results and the greatest level of consistency, the Zone System is your best option. However, it does take a great deal of time and testing to learn, and I must also point out that my description here of the system is only a bare-bones outline. For more information on the Zone System, I recommend finding a book specifically on the subject. A number of books on view cameras also include excellent information on the Zone System, as many large format photographers use it for precise exposures.

that spotmeters are best suited to landscapes and still photography, where you can take the time required to make numerous readings and determine the desired exposure.

Flashmeters. Unlike standard meters, flashmeters are designed to work specifically with flashes. On some models, you use the meter to fire your flashes by PC connector and it automatically meters at the same time. On non-cord models, the unit will wait until it detects the flash firing before metering. The only purpose of these meters is to give you the correct exposure with flash equipment—a feat not possible with normal meters.

The greatest advantage of flashmeters is that they allow photographers to avoid messy guide number calculations and allow the use of more creative lighting. While incredibly useful tools, flashmeters are not suited for general photography. Flashmeters are primarily studio tools, or used in set situations such as location portraiture. If you do any significant studio work with flash, a flashmeter is an essential item to own. However, if you only rarely shoot in the studio or with flash, then a pure flashmeter is an expensive toy you should avoid.

On the other hand, many current flashmeters also function as ambient or spotmeters, making them far less limited. For most general use, a straight hand-held meter offers all you need, but in those instances where you need flashmetering, combination flash/standard meters work perfectly and avoid the need for a separate flashmeter. While these combination meters tend to be more expensive, they are extremely accurate for both flash and standard use. The Minolta Autometer IVf, for example, works as a flashmeter, ambient meter, and reflective meter with the option to use 5° and 10° spot attachments. It is accurate to $1/10$ stop. Such versatility and accuracy is standard with most combination meters, and makes them very useful

tools. If you do occasional flash work or want to eliminate the need for a second dedicated flashmeter, these combination meters are well worth the added cost.

□ Conclusion

When considering accessories for medium format, the key is to make sure you have all the basics covered, and that the accessories you buy fit your needs and your equipment. For long exposures, make sure you have a good tripod and a meter capable of giving you accurate exposure times. In general, most photographers already have the necessary accessories, but take care to make sure you have everything you need before heading out into the field, and that your accessories are appropriate to your medium format equipment, and not merely a 35mm system.

□ Meterless Exposure

Sunny-16 Rule. The Sunny-16 rule is a very useful exposure technique to keep in mind. This rule will give you a good general exposure when shooting outside during the day. Simply stated, exposure under sunny conditions is calculated by the following equation:

$$\text{Exposure} = 1/(\text{film speed}) \text{ seconds at f16}$$

Since film speed rarely matches an actual shutter speed, use the closest possible shutter speed. Thus, if you are shooting a landscape with 100 speed film, your exposure would be $1/125$ second at f16. Under partly cloudy conditions, open up one stop for an exposure of $1/125$ second at f11. Under cloudy conditions, open up two stops for an exposure of $1/125$ second at f8. Naturally, you can adjust aperture and shutter speed to equivalent times to change depth of field or use a particular shutter speed. Thus, your original reading of $1/125$ second at f16 under sunny skies could be adjusted to $1/60$ second at f22, $1/250$ second at f11, $1/500$ second at f8, or any other equivalent exposure time.

While not an exact measurement and only useful outdoors, the Sunny-16 rule provides a surprisingly accurate exposure time in many circumstances. Exposures taken outside using this method will usually result in exposure within one stop of a perfect exposure—within the exposure latitude of most print films to obtain a decent print.

If you use the method exclusively for a few weeks, you will also find yourself developing a sixth sense about exposure times, allowing you to make fairly accurate guesses under various lighting conditions. You can also become a reasonably good guesser at exposure times—very useful in case you forget your meter, or your meter reading seems a bit strange.

Chapter 3
The Twin Lens Reflex

In many respects, the TLR camera is to medium format what the Pentax K-1000 is to 35mm. Of all medium format cameras, the twin lens reflex is by far the most popular starting point for moving into medium format, just as the Pentax K-1000 is one of the most popular entry-level 35mm cameras ever produced. Their availability, relatively small size and light weight (compared to most other medium format cameras), as well as the affordable prices, make TLRs an excellent choice for both amateur and low-cost professional use.

At first glance, the idea of looking through one lens to focus and compose, while taking the actual photograph through another lens may seem a bit strange—yet the design has been well proven over time. Both professionals and amateurs alike have used TLR cameras to produce some of the world's finest images, and for many years the TLR was the camera of choice for press photographers. It was not until the 1960s, with the rise of Nikon and Hasselblad, that the TLR began to lose popularity. Yet, the quality and portability of the twin-lens design has kept these cameras popular in medium format. Many amateurs and professionals still use their Rolleiflex and Mamiya TLR cameras, and continue to produce exceptional images rivaling the best modern SLR equipment.

☐ The Anatomy of a TLR

The distinctive feature of the TLR is the use of two separate lenses, one viewing lens to compose your photograph, and one lens for taking the picture. The advantage of this design is that the taking lens uses a leaf shutter lens (allowing for flash synchronization at all speeds on models with a flash connection), complete lack of vibration when taking the picture, and continuous viewing of the subject during and after exposure. However, there is one important disadvantage: parallax—a topic that is covered in detail below.

Focusing a TLR is achieved by moving the front plate of the camera. This moves both the taking and viewing lenses and ensures that they focus at the same distance. If the front plate of the camera is bent, the viewing and taking lenses will be misaligned and not focus properly. Additionally, a bent front plate could also mean the taking lens is no longer parallel to the film plane, causing additional problems with image sharpness. When considering a TLR, it is critical to make sure the front plate is not bent before using it.

Film is advanced either by knob or crank, usually on the right side of the camera. Depending on the camera, it may automatically advance the film to the next frame, or you may have to use the old red-window system to correctly space each frame.

☐ The Problem of Parallax

Because the viewing lens is above the taking lens, you will not see in the viewfinder exactly what the taking lens records on film. The fact that the lenses are parallel to each other means that the framing inaccuracy is only in vertical orientation, but that is of little comfort when carefully framing a portrait only to find the taking lens cut off the top of your subject's head on the actual film frame. This framing error, referred to as parallax, can create difficulties in any photograph where your subject is less than fifteen feet away. Beyond fifteen feet, the error is marginal, since the view of the taking and viewing lenses overlap sufficiently to eliminate problems. At infinity, the parallax still exists, but is too small to appear in any photograph. At distances under seven feet, parallax can cause major problems.

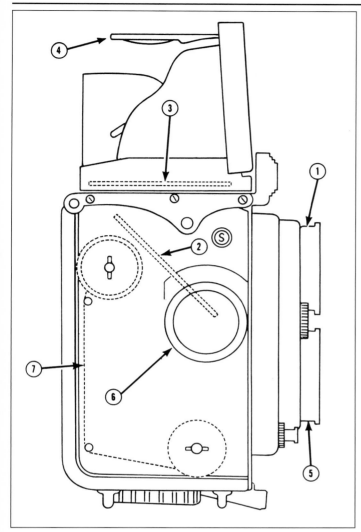

1. Viewing lens. 2. Light passing through the viewing lens hits the mirror angled to reflect it on viewing screen above. 3. Viewing screen. 4. Pop-up magnifier attached to hood aids with focusing. 5. Taking lens. 6. Focusing knob. 7. Film unrolls from spool, passes behind taking lens. Diagram courtesy of Yashica.

Unless you have a Mamiya TLR mounted on a tripod with the Paramender accessory, or a Rollei TLR offering automatic parallax compensation, parallax cannot be eliminated. However, it can be reduced by moving the taking lens into the approximate location of the viewing lens. If you are hand-holding, you can raise the taking lens to the approximate position of the taking lens when you framed the photograph. While not a precise method, it can provide decent compensation with a little practice.

The other method is to mount the camera on a tripod, and raise the taking lens into the position of the viewing lens. To do so, measure the distance from the top of the taking lens to the top of the viewing lens. This is the amount by which you will have to raise the camera to put the taking lens in the position of the viewing lens. After framing with the viewing lens, raise the camera by the amount measured and take your photograph. This method works best on tripods with geared center columns, and when the camera is kept relatively level. On tripods with smooth center columns, you may have to pan the camera to realign the proper framing. If the camera is not level (ie., tilted significantly forward or backward) this method will not work, and will result in framing error.

□ Rotating-Mount Filters

A problem related to parallax is the use of filters with rotating mounts, such as a polarizer. Because the taking lens is separate from the viewing lens, you must first adjust the effect on the viewing lens and then somehow transfer and align the filter properly on the taking lens to get the desired result. With screw thread lenses and filters, this can be particularly irksome, but with practice you can accurately transfer the filter from viewing lens to taking lens (generally by using a pencil or marker of some sort to mark correct positioning on the filter before transferring it to the taking lens). However, since many TLR cameras copied Rollei's bayonet mount, transferring filters can be much easier. Simply set the effect on the viewing lens, and then snap the filter off and onto the taking lens. As long as you are careful not to rotate the filter when transferring it, you will obtain the exact effect you desire. In the end, the filter issue is more of an annoyance than a true problem with the TLR design and is not an issue with standard colored filters. In fact, with colored filters, focusing and framing can be easier, as the filter is not reducing the light coming into the viewfinder as it does on an SLR.

□ Getting the Most Out of a TLR

Since most TLR cameras are in 6x6 format, negatives are very easy to work with. You not only have the choice of full-frame square images, but also extensive cropping abilities, should you use standard print sizes such as 8"x10". This allows for a bit more freedom when taking photographs, as you don't have to worry about turning the camera to get a vertical

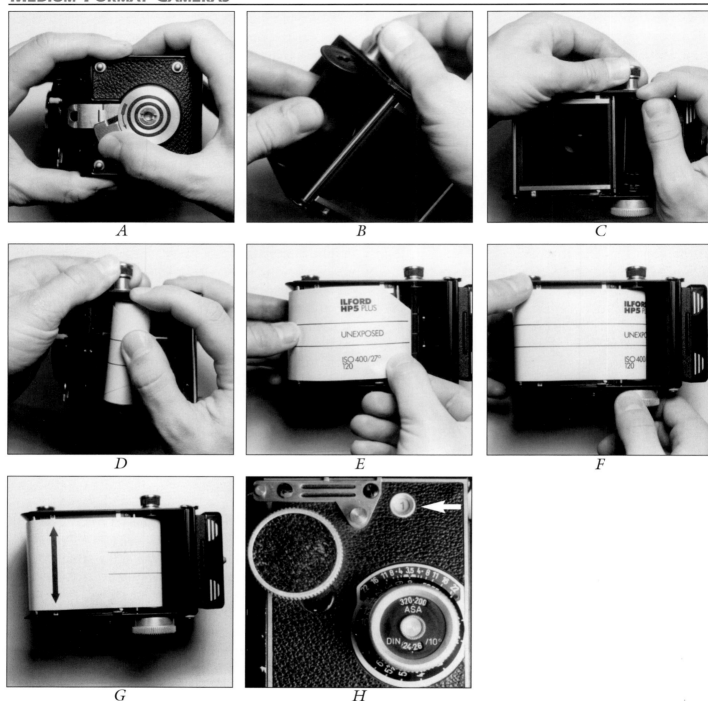

Loading a TLR: A) Unlock and open the camera. B) Remove the old film spool from the bottom position—this will be your new take-up spool. C) Insert the take-up spool in the upper position. D) Insert the new roll of film in the bottom position. E) Carefully pull the film over the rollers and insert it into the take-up spool. Make sure the black surface is facing towards the lens. F) Once securely loaded into the take-up spool, advance the film. G) Once the arrows on the back of the film line up with the red dots or arrows in the film chamber, close the back. H) Once the camera back is closed and locked, advance the camera until the counter reads one. On "red window" cameras, look through the red window until you see a "1" appear. NOTE: On Rolleiflex cameras, you must be careful to load the film under the first roller, and close the back immediately after you see the arrows on the film appear. This is due to the automatic film sensor in the Rolleiflex cameras, which will automatically sense when the film starts and set the advance system accordingly.

shot. You can simply compose, shoot, and crop in the darkroom—yet another reason (beyond cost and weight issues) for the popularity of the cameras with beginning medium format photographers.

Another tremendous, and often overlooked, advantage of twin lens cameras is the waist-level find-

The waist-level finder is standard on most TLR cameras, and includes a magnifier to assist in focusing. When holding the camera, make sure you support the camera from underneath with one hand, and use the other for focusing and releasing the shutter. This will help keep the camera stable and, with practice, you should be able to take sharp photos at speeds of $^1/_{15}$ second or even $^1/_8$ second. For most photos, the magnifier is recommended because it makes focusing and framing a bit easier, but you can also hold the camera at your waist for more relaxed shooting. Find yourself stuck in a crowd? You can flip the camera upside down, hold it above your head, and focus and frame you photo. This "periscope" method is a great advantage of the waist-level finder, and is particularly useful at parades and other crowded situations.

er standard on the majority of TLR cameras. When holding the camera at your waist or even bringing it up to your eye, people have a tendency to believe you are fiddling with the camera, not taking a photo. In social situations, this can allow you to obtain more candid images—one reason why a number of wedding photographers still use and prefer a TLR over other camera types. For the same reason, a TLR can work extremely well for street photography.

TLR cameras also work extremely well for general photography. In any situation where a manual 35mm camera would be appropriate, a TLR can work just as well, but will give you the advantage of the larger negative. Landscapes, for example, are an excellent use for a TLR; the larger negative and relatively small size and weight makes them excellent medium format cameras for field use. Because of the leaf shutter, twin-lens cameras are also near silent, making them ideal for situations where the loud flop of a mirror or whir of a motor would be unacceptable (such as at a concert or stage play).

While some may consider the fixed 75mm or 80mm lens on most TLR cameras a disadvantage, the lens is equivalent to a 45mm lens on a 35mm camera. I have heard some photographers comment that a standard lens (45mm–55mm range) is dull—one even going so far as to suggest they belong in the trash. However, this could not be further from the truth. Since the 45mm is considered the closest lens in 35mm to the angle of view of the human eye, TLR cameras are capable of very natural-looking photographs with their fixed 75mm or 80mm lens. Personally, I find a standard lens indispensable for general use and low-light photography, since standard lenses often have faster maximum apertures than wide angle or telephoto lenses. Many of the world's greatest photographs were taken with TLR cameras (particularly Rolleiflex), further proving that the fixed lens should not be considered a limitation. In fact, many photographers would see vast improvement in their work if they limited themselves to one lens and learned to produce excellent photographs with it. In many cases, the mark of a top photographer is the ability to use extremely limited equipment and still produce the finest results.

With TLR cameras such as the Rolleiflex with Planar or Xenotar lens, and the Mamiya C-series, twin-lens cameras are not limited to only amateur or entry-level use. The best TLR cameras will

Many TLR cameras also offer a sportsfinder for fast action photography. While using the sportsfinder, there is usually no provision to check focus, so it must be done by scale (read: guesswork). For quick framing and shooting, the sportsfinder can be useful.

produce results that will match the best modern equipment, but often at a fraction of the cost of a new medium format SLR. A Rolleiflex with Planar lens, for example, can be found for under $400 where a used Hasselblad with Planar lens could easily cost you $1000—with no discernable increase in image quality. In short, TLRs provide both an excellent starting and ending point for medium format equipment, provided you can accept the occasional parallax difficulties.

☐ Rolleiflex and Rolleicord

The Rolls Royce of TLRs. One the most recognized names in photography, Rollei's long history in medium format TLR cameras begins in 1932 with the original Rolleiflex. Since the introduction of that camera, Rollei earned one of the best reputations for exceptional quality equipment, and even the earliest equipment is still extremely well regarded and sought after by both photographers and collectors.

For those looking at Rolleiflex and Rolleicord cameras, the task can seem a bit daunting due to the tremendous number of models produced—there are over fifty TLR models and variations. Making matters even more challenging is the fact that the differ-

ences between many of the models are minor, and there is even variation within specific models. Identifying exactly which model you have requires matching the serial number and features to the list offered in a collector's guide.

Taking Lens. When taking a look at Rollei TLR cameras, the first item you should look at is the taking lens. Of all the features of the camera, this is by far the most important in relation to image quality, and also the most significant factor in determining the value of the camera. The latest Rolleiflex model with 80mm f2.8 Zeiss Planar lens can cost a fortune, while the older cameras with f3.5 Xenar or Tessar lenses command much more modest sums.

For most general photography, models with coated Xenar or Tessar lens work exceptionally well. Both lenses offer excellent sharpness and resolution, and are bested only by the top modern lenses or the later Planar and Xenotar models. This excellent image quality, combined with the solid construction found

Rolleicord V, with multiple exposures, MXV sync, and superb Schneider Xenar lens.

in Rollei TLR cameras, makes them excellent candidates for both entry-level and serious photography. Models with these lenses can be found for $175–275 in excellent working order (less for some Rolleicords).

If you require the sharpest lens possible or if you plan to make sizable enlargements (16"x20" or larger), you will want to look into the Planar or Xenotar models. These cameras offer top-notch performance capable of matching the best of modern lenses, and as such tend to command heftier prices. Earlier cameras with the 75mm f3.5 lenses can be found for $350 or so, with later models fetching over $1000. Since 80mm f2.8 models are even more desirable, few will be found for less than $550—and the latest 2.8GX fetches $3500 new.

At these prices, the Planar and Xenotar models represent significant investments, and you may wish to look at a Mamiya C-series TLR with interchangeable lenses or an SLR system before committing to a Rolleiflex in this range. While excellent cameras with top-notch optics, the fixed lens may be limiting in the long run, unless you prefer the simplicity and quality of the fixed-lens Rollei.

Flash Sync. Beyond the taking lens, consider other features you may need. If you use flash, make sure you obtain a Rollei with flash sync. The shutter will be marked "Syncro-Compur" for models with flash sync, and the flash will be connected by PC cord (except on the latest models with TTL flash, which have hot shoes). Shutters with MX sync allow the use of flashbulbs when set to the "M" position.

Self Timer. On cameras with MXV sync, the "V" setting is self timer (approximately ten seconds). Other Rollei's with self timers will have a switch on the top left of the focusing plate above and to the left of the viewing lens. To use the timer on Rolleicord models and those with distinct MXV switches, make sure the shutter is set, and then arm the self-timer by moving the switch over or putting the sync switch in "V." When you press the shutter release, the self timer will activate and fire the shutter after a ten second delay. On Rolleiflex models with the timer switch above the viewing lens, the timer will begin to run immediately after you flip the timer switch, and will set off the shutter after about ten seconds.

Multiple Exposures. Multiple exposures are also possible on a large number of models. On Rolleiflex

models with this option, there is a knurled catch underneath where the wind crank connects to the camera; turn it to "multi," and then turn the crank backwards to set the shutter without advancing the film. On later Rolleicord models, there is a switch to allow for multiple exposures; when the red dot is showing, you may cock the shutter and take as many exposures as you wish.

Other Features. Later models also have more provisions for accessories. Starting with models that feature the f3.5 Xenotar and Planar lens, built-in meters are available. The latest models also offer modern comforts such as removable hoods and interchangeable focusing screens, while offering technological advances such as TTL flashmetering.

> *"The latest models also offer modern comforts such as removable hoods..."*

Filters and Accessories. For filters and other accessories, Rollei cameras feature a bayonet system, rather than a threaded filter ring. Besides offering faster mounting of filters, you can also view the effect of a polarizer (or similar rotating-mount filter) and then snap the filter onto the taking lens with perfect assurance that you will obtain the effect you desire. Thanks to companies—such as Yashica—who have copied the Rollei bayonets, filters, wide angle and telephoto adaptors, as well as other accessories, are easier to find. The bayonet sizes vary from Bay I to Bay IV. Bay I is used for Tessar, Triotar, Xenar, and late Baby Rollei 4x4 models, Bay II for f3.5 Planar and Xenotar models, Bay III for all f2.8 and Tele Rolleiflex models, and Bay IV for the Rollei Wide.

35mm photography is also possible in Rollei cameras by using the Rolleikin adaptor kit. This kit consists of a take-up spool and masking plate to allow for 35mm film (24 exposures only). However, to use the Rolleikin kit you need to have a Rollei TLR with switchable film pressure plate that will accommodate the kit. Also included in the kit is an auxiliary film counter for 35mm, which is required for most Rollei models taking the Rolleikin.

One of the best features found on Rollei TLR cameras is parallax compensation. Unlike most other TLR cameras, which offer no compensation whatsoever for distances under twenty feet, Rollei included a pair of sliding metal plates in the viewfinder that adjust with focusing distance. These plates adjust the image in the viewfinder to correct for parallax, which means no special accessories are required. Also, with the exception of the f2.8 models, the viewing lens has a wider aperture than the taking lens, which provides a brighter viewfinder image.

☐ **Serial Numbers**

For serial number buffs, look for Rolleiflex f3.5 models with serial numbers higher than 1,100,000, Rolleicords with serial numbers higher than 1,137,000, or any f2.8 model. These models will offer coated lenses and x-sync at the very least, and the vast majority will have adjustable pressure plates for use with the Rolleikin adaptors.

Rolleiflex or Rolleicord? While the Rolleiflex models generally garner the greatest attention, the Rolleicords cannot be overlooked. Deciding between the two comes down to a matter of convenience and lens selection more than actual construction quality. While the Rolleicord was sold as a lower-cost alternative to the full Rolleiflex, there are only two major differences between them.

First, you must manually cock the shutter on Rolleicord models, while the Rolleiflex automatically cocks the shutter when the film is advanced. (The earliest Rolleiflex models are the only exception—like the Rolleicords, you must cock the shutter manually on these. All Rolleiflexes manufactured after 1937 (the vast majority) will cock automatically when the film is advanced.) Second, the Rolleiflex uses a crank to advance the film, while the Rolleicord has a knob. These differences make the Rolleiflex slightly faster and easier to work with, but the extra speed and efficiency of the Rolleiflex won't be a significant factor with most general photography— only in action situations will it make any sort of difference.

Given this, Rolleicord models can be exceptional bargains. For example, a Rolleicord V with Xenar lens and MXV sync can be found for $175 or so. To get the same lens and features in a Rolleiflex, the price jumps to about $250. For entry-level medium format, or those on a tight budget who still want Rollei quality, Rolleicord models should be seriously considered.

The largest disadvantage to the Rolleicord series is the lack of availability of the later lenses. While Rolleicord models were produced until 1975, they were never upgraded to the Planar or Xenotar lens in keeping with their position as low-cost alternatives to the full Rolleiflex models. Thus, the Rolleicord models are limited more to amateur use or entry-level medium format, whereas the later Rolleiflex models offer image quality on par with the latest SLR lenses.

Overall, Rollei TLR cameras represent some of the best values in medium format today. With their combination of features, reliability, and top-quality optics even from vintage cameras, Rollei has earned a well-deserved reputation in photography. For both entry-level and serious medium format photography, Rollei must be considered.

Lenses. *Carl Zeiss or Schneider-Kreuznach?* When looking at Rollei TLR cameras, those models with Zeiss lenses seem to be more desirable. Prices are slightly higher than on variations with a Schneider lens, and photographers always extol the virtues of Zeiss lenses. There are also some vague notions that Zeiss quality control and design was better, but these are unsubstantiated rumors; the Schneider Xenar and Zeiss Tessar lenses are virtually identical in design, and the Schneider Xenotar and Zeiss Planar are likewise very similar. In large part, the rumors are due to Zeiss' long-standing (and well-deserved) reputation around the world for high-quality optics, and greater name recognition in the United States. However, it should be remembered that, while perhaps not quite as well-known in the United States, Schneider has also been producing some of the world's finest lenses for decades, and is currently an industry leader in large format lenses.

In selecting lenses and lens manufacturers for their cameras, Rollei made sure to buy lenses from only the best manufacturers. Thus, you can rest assured that both the Schneider and Zeiss lenses are excellent performers, and neither is significantly better than the other on cameras of the same vintage. In fact, you can sometimes use this fact to your advantage. Because collectors and brand-conscious buyers prefer the Zeiss models, they tend to be more desirable and command a premium. You can often haggle a bit more when you find a Rollei with a Schneider lens, and acquire the same level of quality without the added premium the Zeiss name can cause.

The following lenses are commonly found on Rollei TLR cameras.

Zeiss Triotar Lens (75mm f4.5 or f3.5). A good three-element lens used only with Rolleicord models, the Triotar is better than a number of lenses found on vintage folding cameras and other inexpensive TLRs, making it a good option for those on a budget. Performance will not match that of a Xenar, Tessar, or later lens, but the Triotar is still a good design and can offer acceptable results, particularly in black and white.

Zeiss Tessar (75mm f3.8 or f4.5 on the earliest models, 75mm f3.5 on later models). Well regarded by photographers and collectors, the Zeiss Tessar is an excellent lens, and also the one that helped Rollei earn its reputation for superior image quality. The earliest Rolleiflex cameras used Tessar lenses, although they were either f3.8 or f4.5 and not the updated f3.5 version seen on later cameras. In medium format, coated versions of the f3.5 Tessar are still considered a standard of comparison, a testament to the excellent design and quality offered by Zeiss. Any Rollei with a Tessar lens is desirable, and will produce excellent photographs. In fact, only the best modern lenses or later Planar/Xenotar models provide significant improvement in image quality. However, for improved color performance, the later coated versions are recommended over earlier uncoated lenses.

It should be noted that there is also an 80mm f2.8 Zeiss Tessar found only on the first Rolleiflex 2.8 models. Interestingly enough, the first Rolleiflexes to feature this lens were recalled as the original lenses, produced before or during World War II, were found to be substandard. Most cameras were refitted with improved Tessar lenses produced after the war, although a small number still have the original lenses.

Schneider Xenar (75mm f3.5). The Xenar lens is nearly identical in design and performance to the Zeiss Tessar, making it another solid option to consider. Rollei began using the Xenar after World War II, because the Carl Zeiss Jena factory, in Russian-occupied Germany, could not supply sufficient quantities of the Tessar. It would eventually replace the Zeiss Triotar as the standard lens for Rolleicord cameras, starting with the Rolleicord IV.

Zeiss Planar (75mm f3.5 and 80mm f2.8). First introduced in 1954 on the 2.8C model, the Planar design represented a significant improvement over the older Tessar and Xenar lenses. In 1956, the Planar design was ported to the f3.5 series cameras, and would become the standard lens for later Rolleiflex cameras. Starting sometime in the mid-1960s, a weak sixth element was added to the 75mm lens to improve performance (although most find the improvement barely noticeable). The Planar lens is a truly excellent design, and can often outperform even the latest lenses in color, resolution, and contrast. As a result, Planar lens models are highly sought after by photographers and command significantly higher prices than earlier models.

"The performance of the Schneider lens is very close to that of the Zeiss Planar..."

Schneider Xenotar (75mm f3.5 and 80mm f2.8). On later Rolleiflex models, the Xenotar is to the Planar what the Xenar is to the Tessar. The design and performance of the Schneider lens is very close to that of the Zeiss Planar, making it a very desirable lens (particularly the 80mm f2.8 models). Like the Planar, its optical performance ranks it up with the best modern lenses. The Xenotar should be considered a truly serious photographic tool.

Zeiss aficionados will also be interested to know that the Xenotar was introduced before the Planar, and it was only after extensive testing that Rollei began to use the Planar design in addition to the Xenotar, a testament to the quality of both lenses.

Zeiss-Jena Biometar (80mm f2.8). Seen only on the f2.8B model, the Zeiss Jena Biometar was produced by the East German Zeiss-Jena factory. Produced for Rollei only in 1952 and 1953 for the f2.8B, this is the last Zeiss-Jena lens to be offered on a Rollei TLR. All later Zeiss lenses came from Carl Zeiss in West Germany. The Biometar is a solid lens, capable of truly excellent performance. It should also be noted that the Biometar was used on Exacta, Kiev, and other East German/Russian cameras, and has an excellent reputation for image quality.

☐ Mamiya C-Series TLRs
Interchangeable Lenses. Unlike the vast majority of TLR cameras, the Mamiya twin-lens cameras offer a complete system of interchangeable lenses and find-

ers. To my knowledge, the only other TLR cameras to offer interchangeable lenses are the rare Koni-Omegaflex and 4x5 Gowlandflex cameras. With lenses available from 55mm to 250mm, and a wide range of accessories, the Mamiya cameras are extremely versatile. Additionally, since they were designed and constructed for professional use, they are well built and extremely reliable.

☐ **More on Mamiya**

For complete information on these excellent cameras, I suggest you take a look at Graham Patterson's Mamiya TLR FAQ on the Internet. He has compiled the most complete set of information on the cameras and accessories, and it is well worth a look if you are interested in buying a Mamiya TLR. It is located at <http://www.btinternet.com/~g.a.patterson/m_faq.htm>.

Finders and Accessories. The list of available finders and accessories is quite extensive, and makes the cameras more desirable. You can find various metered finders, non-metered finders, hand grips, and even a sheet film adaptor. Mamiya also produced a series of Paramenders, which would eliminate parallax when the camera was mounted on a tripod. This accessory is a must if you do any close-up work or tight head shots, and is the only TLR camera to my knowledge to offer such a valuable accessory. In all, the list of accessories is quite impressive in keeping with the original intention of the cameras as professional tools.

Bodies. The following sections provide detail on specific Mamiya TLR bodies.

Mamiyaflex C. The original body in the Mamiya TLR series, it was introduced in 1957 with three lenses—an 80mm f2.8, 105mm f3.5, and 135mm f4.5. Film advance is done by knob, and the shutter must be cocked before each exposure. Focusing is accomplished using a knob on the bottom right of the camera, and the camera has double exposure prevention.

Mamiyaflex C2. Introduced only a year after the original Mamiyaflex C, the C2 is essentially the same camera, except with focusing knobs on both sides of the camera making life a bit easier for left-handed photographers. The camera was also introduced with two new lenses—65mm and 180mm.

Mamiya C3. In 1962, the Mamiyaflex was completely redesigned and the C3 Professional was intro-

duced. It featured a wind crank rather than an advance knob, automatic double exposure prevention (with a switch for multiple exposures), and the counter resets automatically, making film handling easier. At the same time, all the lenses were upgraded to feature shutters with a ¹⁄₅₀₀ second top speed.

Mamiya C33. Introduced in 1965, the C33 added automatic shutter cocking when the film was advanced. An automatic parallax indicator was added, and 220 film could be used by changing to a different film back cover. However, it should be noted that not all C33 models can take the 220 option—the earliest versions are not able to mount the 220 cover and cannot be modified to take it. In many respects, the C33 is the same as the later C330, except that it is noticeably heavier, and has depth of field scales for the older chrome lenses.

Mamiya C22. Introduced as a lighter, lower cost option to the C33, the C22 is essentially the same as the earlier C2, except with the addition of the automatic double-exposure prevention.

Mamiya C220. Introduced in 1968, the C220 is essentially a stripped-down version of the C330 cam-

Mamiya C330 Professional TLR, shown with an older 80mm f2.8 Chrome lens.

eras. It is slightly smaller and lighter than the C330, and has virtually the same features of the C3 Professional. Film advance is achieved by a knob with fold-out crank. Since the viewfinder only covers the 80mm lens, accessory masks must be used when longer lenses are used. At the same time as the C220 was introduced, the 55mm and 250mm lenses were also introduced.

Mamiya C330. Introduced a year after the C220, the C330 offers many improvements over previous models. The automatic parallax compensation was upgraded to also provide exposure compensation data to take the bellows factor into account. A distance-scale rod and interchangeable focusing screens were also introduced. The camera offers 120/220 capability by adjusting the film pressure plate.

Lenses. Mamiya TLR lenses are available in focal lengths from 55mm up to 250mm, which covers the majority of all photographic situations. Each lens set is comprised of the exact same lens for viewing and taking. This gives an added bonus—should something happen to your taking lens (scratch, chip, etc.), you can sometimes swap in the cells from the viewing lens and use the damaged taking lens for viewing. However, this should be done by a repair technician to ensure that the lenses are properly calibrated, and to also make sure that it is possible to exchange cells. It is not a recommended procedure, but can be useful to know in case you find yourself in a bind.

Lenses for the Mamiya TLR are well designed and still in use by professional photographers, particularly the later black-series lenses. All lenses are coated and give solid color performance. Flash sync with the built-in leaf shutter is available at all speeds by standard PC connection. There is a switch on the lens to choose X sync for standard electronic flash and "M" for bulb flashes.

To change a lens, first make sure the bellows is fully racked into the camera. Then locate the knob on the left side of the camera and move it to the *lock* position. You can now open the wire retaining lock and remove the lens. Mount the new lens, and lock the retaining wire back into position. Now turn the knob on back to the *unlock* position, and you're ready to go.

Chrome ($1/400$ second top speed). These lenses are the first made for the Mamiya TLR cameras. They are identified by the chrome shutter speed dial and

barrel, and a $1/400$ second top speed on the Seikosha-MX shutter. Because of their age and lower top speed, these lenses are less desirable than later lenses.

Chrome (later series). These lenses are identical in look to the earlier chrome lenses, but have a top speed of $1/500$ second with the Seikosha-S shutter. The only difference between these lenses and the older models is the shutter—optically, they are the same. Please note that some chrome series lenses do have black trim, but should not be confused with the later black lenses. If the shutter speed dial is chrome, the lens is *not* from the later black series. There are five lenses available in this series—65mm f3.5, 80mm f2.8, 105mm f3.5, 135mm f4.5, and 180mm f4.5.

Black Series. The latest lenses for the Mamiya TLR cameras are easily identified—the barrel of the lens is black, as is the shutter speed dial. All the lenses were redesigned, giving improved performance over the older versions. As a result, these lenses are the most desirable, and will cost more than earlier lenses. There are ten black lenses available—55mm f4.5, 65mm f3.5, 80mm f2.8, 80mm f3.7 (rare budget version of the 80mm f2.8 with Copal shutter that must be cocked manually for each exposure), 105mm f3.5, 105mm f3.5 D/DS (with aperture in taking lens to preview depth of field), 135mm f4.5, 180mm f4.5, 180mm f4.5 Super, and 250mm f6.3 (must be manually cocked before each exposure).

> "To change a lens, first make sure the bellows is fully racked into the camera."

Finders. The following finders are featured on Mamiya TLR cameras.

Waist-Level Finder (WLF). Standard waist level viewer with magnifier. Most have a sportsfinder built-in, but some do not.

Porrofinder. Essentially, the Porrofinder is a pentaprism with offset viewer. It can be found both in metered and non-metered versions.

Prism. Allows focusing though a standard prism, like those on an SLR. The image is brighter than that of the Porrofinder, but the prism is also significantly heavier.

Chimney or Magnifying Viewer. This viewer operates like a WLF, but has a magnified view. Available in both metered and non-metered versions.

☐ *Yashica TLRs*

Beyond the Rollei and Mamiya TLRs, the Yashicas are the next–best-known cameras, and have become one of the most popular starting points in medium format photography, due to their good quality and excellent prices. A Yashica D, for example, can often be purchased for $100 or less in excellent condition. The Yashica cameras also reveal one insight into TLR cameras in general—most manufacturers then (and those producing TLRs now) attempted to copy Rollei's camera designs, with variable success. Using the same bayonet filter mount and copying the thumb wheels found on Rolleiflex cameras to adjust shutter and aperture, the Yashica cameras look very similar to the more expensive Rolleis.

In comparison to Rollei and Mamiya, the Yashicas are not as well built, nor do they have the same image quality. While some have said the four-element Yashinon lens used on the Yashica-Mat models can match the quality of a Rollei, my own experience with a Yashica-Mat 124-G (the last Yashica TLR produced) did not confirm this. While the lens was exceptionally sharp in the center of the negative and certainly matched that of the Xenar on my Rolleicord, the corners were a bit soft. Others I have spoken to have had similar results—but it should be noted that the lens performance was still quite good and negatives from the camera could provide decent 11"x14" enlargements. Because of the excellent center sharpness, the Yashinon lens is very capable as a portrait lens, where slight softness in the corners is not a problem and can actually be an advantage in blurring the background. The three-element Yashikor lens found on the less expensive models isn't quite as good as the Yashinon, but is still quite capable of producing good quality negatives and is hard to beat in regard to bang for the buck.

For entry-level medium format and serious amateur use on a budget, Yashica cameras should be seriously considered. However, I do recommend avoid-

Yashica TLRs. Photo courtesy of Yashica.

ing the Yashica-Mat 124-G as prices for that camera have become inflated beyond reasonable levels. At the current cost of the 124-G, you could easily find a Rolleiflex (possibly a good user with Xenotar lens). For those on a budget, the too often overlooked Yashica A and D models combine excellent value with solid performance.

Models and Features. *Yashica A.* The most inexpensive of all the Yashica TLR cameras, it comes with the three-element Yashikor lens and a shutter with speeds from $1/25$ second to $1/300$ second, plus B and X sync. Film advance is manual using the red-window system, and the shutter must be cocked before each exposure. Because of the manual film advance and limited shutter speeds, this camera is not particularly valuable and can be obtained for $50 or less—making it a great bargain for inexpensive entry into medium format.

Yashica B. Very similar to the Yashica A, but using levers on either side of the lens to adjust shutter and aperture.

Yashica C. Shutter speeds are expanded to one second through $1/300$, and a semi-automatic film advance is offered. To advance the film, press a button on the advance knob, then advance the film. The camera automatically sets the correct frame spacing, and will lock the knob when the next frame is reached (making life a bit easier than with the red-window system of the A and B models). The lens is Yashikor, and offers XM sync.

Yashica D. An upgrade over the C model, the shutter has speeds from one second to $1/500$, plus B, timer, and MX sync. As with the Yashica C, the shutter must be cocked manually before each exposure. Later models feature the better Yashinon lens.

Yashica E. A somewhat rare model, this was the only Yashica TLR to offer autoexposure (similar to the rare Rolleimagic models from Rollei). These cameras are not recommended for actual use, as there is no provision for manual exposure control, and the autoexposure system and meter is questionable (particularly given the age of all these cameras).

Yashica LM. The earliest Yashica TLR with a meter, it also offers semiautomatic film advance, as seen on the C and D models, but is only found with the early three-element lenses.

Yashica 635. The 635 is one of the more interesting models in the Yashica line. Originally featuring the three-element Yashikor lens, this camera was designed as a dual-format camera. It takes both 120 film for 6x6 but also 35mm in 20 or 36 exposures. Like the Yashica D, film advance is semi-automatic and offers the same range of shutter speeds, flash sync, and self timer, and later models may offer the better Yashinon lens. The only difficulty with this model is finding a camera with complete 35mm adaptor kit.

Yashica-Mat. With the four-element Yashinon lens, this camera is one to look for. In addition to the better lens, the camera also automatically cocks the shutter when the film is advanced, just like a Rolleiflex. The Copal shutter offers speeds from one second to $1/500$ second, plus B and MX flash sync. In all-around value, the Yashica-Mat is probably the best in the line, as it offers all the significant upgrades in lens and body (except for 220 capability, which most photographers rarely use), and a built-in meter.

> # "...it's an interesting model and the only Yashica to offer autoexposure."

Yashica-Mat LM. Essentially, the LM is a regular Yashica-Mat, but with an added uncoupled exposure meter sensitive from ISO 6 to 400. By today's standards, this is not a great ISO range for the meter, but in its day it was top technology and still covers the majority of film speeds commonly used (ISO 100 and 400).

Yashica-Mat EM. Similar to the LM, but with different meter configuration.

Yashica 24. The first of the "modern" Yashicas, it offered the better Yashinon lens. Furthermore, it has a built-in meter that is coupled to the shutter and aperture, offering match needle metering. The only drawback is that it only takes 220 film, and is somewhat hard to find.

Yashica 12. Introduced after the Yashica 24, the Yashica 12 is the same camera but takes only 120 film. For those looking for a Yashica with a coupled meter, it's a good value, as the selling price is generally less than that of the 124 models, but it is also a relatively hard model to find.

Yashicamat 124. The Yashicamat 124 adds switchable 120/220 capability. Otherwise, this camera is pretty much the same as the Yashica 12. This camera provides one of the most inexpensive medi-

Super Ricohflex TLR camera. Manual advance using the "red window" system. Focusing on this camera is unique—unlike most TLR cameras where you focus by knob, you focus this camera by turning either the taking or the viewing lens. The gearing visible around both lenses moves the other lens and ensures the focus is correct. It is the first time I have ever seen a TLR with a dual-helicoid system instead of focus adjustment by moving the entire front plate of the camera. The low-cost nature of the camera is obvious as it uses a cheap box camera-type insert to hold the film, but the 80mm f3.5 Ricoh Anastigmat lens is actually coated, so it provides good contrast and color. Cost: $25. Fun factor: Extremely high.

um format cameras to give 220 capability, and with the built-in meter is an excellent all-in-one TLR at reasonable cost (although prices are starting to get a little inflated for this model—don't pay more than $250).

Yashicamat 124-G. The last Yashica TLR, it remained in production until the mid-1980s, and stores were still selling new cameras into the early 1990s (often at very low prices to get them off the shelves). The only change from the previous 124 was to gold-plate the meter contacts. While a good camera, prices have recently become grossly inflated. If you find one for $250 or less, the 124-G is a good buy; if the price goes over this mark, a Rollei or older Mamiya would be a better option.

Other Models. There were a few other models made, such as the "Yashicaflex" models. Yashica also made a line of TLR cameras using 127 film—they are designated 44 and can be found in a number of different versions. These are not included in this book, as 127 film is no longer readily available.

☐ Other TLRs

While the Mamiya, Rollei, and Yashica cameras are certainly the best known and most widely available, there are a number of other good TLR cameras available. The Minolta Autocord, for example, is a solid camera with optics many consider to be similar in quality to the Xenar and Tessar lenses found on earlier Rollei cameras. Some, like the Ricohflex, are truly unique and interesting cameras to use—images from the Ricoh certainly are not the best but, with its coated taking lens, acceptable prints up to 11"x11" can be made. This camera also adds a certain fun-factor as the geared focusing mechanism connecting the taking and viewing lenses is unlike any other TLR I have ever seen, and the camera uses a film insert system like those seen on old box cameras.

TLR cameras are still in production today, with an abundance of them coming from China. "Great Wall" cameras often show up, although many times under different brand names. As with Russian cameras, the Chinese cameras are highly variable in quality, both optically and mechanically. "Seagull" cameras are perhaps the best known and most widely available of the TLRs currently in production, and many photographers have had reasonable success with them. Their quality does not match that of a Rollei but, like the Yashica models, the Seagulls offer reasonable quality at a good price.

An enduring design, the twin-lens reflex will likely be with us for years to come. By offering excellent quality at reasonable cost, the TLR will also remain a popular choice for medium format photography. For both entry-level and serious professional use, these cameras should be considered—particularly if you find yourself on a budget.

A snapshot from the Ricohflex. Note that the overall resolution of the print is quite good. This print would easily enlarge to 11"x11" or 16"x16" and still look quite good (lackluster composition aside), despite the fact that the camera used would be considered junk when compared to most modern equipment.

Chapter 4

Rangefinder and Viewfinder Cameras

Of all types of cameras, the rangefinder/viewfinder camera is by far the one with which most people are familiar. Virtually every point-and-shoot camera is either a rangefinder or viewfinder camera (one where you focus and/or frame your photograph in a viewfinder separate from the taking lens). Serious photographers are all familiar with Leica rangefinder cameras, perhaps the best known and most widely respected of all rangefinders.

In medium format, rangefinder and viewfinder cameras offer the widest selection of equipment, both in terms of price and quality. From the old Kodak folding cameras to the Mamiya 7-II, there's a camera that will meet the demands of amateurs, professionals, and those simply looking for a fun camera to carry. Rangefinder and viewfinder cameras can also be found for as little as $10 (and with quality that would surprise you). For anyone looking into medium format, these cameras must be considered—with the plethora of folding cameras available for mere peanuts, you can test the waters without costly investment.

☐ Rangefinder vs. Viewfinder

Rangefinder and viewfinder cameras are like apples, but from different trees. Just as all trout are fish, but not all fish are trout, all rangefinder cameras are viewfinder cameras, but not all viewfinder cameras are rangefinders. Both share the same basic design—you frame your photograph through a finder separate from the taking lens, but not a matched lens as seen in the TLR design.

What sets the rangefinder apart from the standard viewfinder camera is the provision for focusing or parallax correction based on distance, hence the "range" in rangefinder. Most rangefinders will

include a coupled rangefinder, by which you can focus the lens. As you adjust the focus on the lens, you will see a double image in the viewfinder. When the two images meet and become a single image, the lens is in focus. This design is generally referred to as the split-image rangefinder, and is by far the most common.

> ## "As you adjust the focus, you will see a double image in the viewfinder."

Where the term "rangefinder" enters a gray area is with cameras that have parallax compensation lines, but no provision for focusing. On the one hand, they have some provision for adjusting framing based on distance, but without a split-image or other focusing system you cannot find the exact distance to your subject and thus they do not give you an exact range. However, it must also be remembered that many split-image rangefinders do not have parallax compensation lines to adjust framing based on distance. As a result, consider any viewfinder camera with parallax compensation lines or some sort of focusing system a rangefinder, as both provide adjustment to either framing or focus based on distance to the subject.

Advantages and Disadvantages. Of all the camera types, viewfinder and rangefinder cameras offer some of the best advantages around, when compared to other cameras. At the same time, though, they feature some of the worst disadvantages. In the end, these merits and flaws tend to balance—yet some of those flaws could completely disqualify you from using a camera of this type. First, the bad news.

Rangefinder and viewfinder cameras offer a wide selection of equipment, both in terms of price and quality.

As seen with TLR design, parallax becomes an issue with any camera that uses a finder system completely separate from the taking lens. With viewfinder cameras, this problem becomes even more of a concern as the viewfinder is often located diagonally away from the taking lens. Thus, where a TLR requires only vertical compensation, a viewfinder camera may require both horizontal and vertical compensation in framing. As a result, viewfinder and rangefinder cameras are often unsuitable for studio or close-up work. Many of the latest rangefinder cameras offer complete parallax compensation, yet they are still limited to a minimum working distance of three to five feet.

Also, like a TLR, using any filter with a rotating mount or variable effect becomes more difficult.

Unlike the TLR, filters cannot be mounted on the viewfinder. Thus, you cannot mount and mark a filter, as on a TLR with viewing lens, and must gauge effect and proper setting for the filter by hand (either holding the filter in front of the viewfinder or simply looking through the filter itself and adjusting). With practice, results can be reasonable, yet the exact effect will be less precise than either a TLR or SLR. However, it should be noted that with standard filters, viewfinder and rangefinder cameras have a distinct advantage. Because you do not have the filter reducing the amount of light entering the viewfinder, focusing is far easier and more accurate than in an SLR.

There is also no viewfinder blackout, as with a SLR when the mirror flips, so you can see your subject at the exact moment the shutter fires. This helps if you are using flash and want to make sure the flash actually fired, or, more importantly, if you are attempting to catch the right expression on your subject's face, as in a wedding photo or portrait. TLRs share these advantages, but the viewfinder or rangefinder camera takes this ability one step farther. With both SLRs and TLRs, ease of focusing is limited by the maximum aperture of the lens through which you view. With a TLR, this may be a relatively bright f2.8 on the viewing lens, but an SLR is limited by the lens in use (which can be anywhere from f2.0 to f8, depending on lens and focal length). A rangefinder camera, on the other hand, can offer a bright, clear view regardless of the aperture of the taking lens as the viewfinder is completely separate. As a result, rangefinders can be faster and infinitely easier to both focus and frame your subject, even under sunny conditions. Leica shooters often state rangefinder focusing is 25% more accurate than any other type of camera, and while I am unsure of how this figure was derived, the fact remains that rangefinders are significantly easier to focus than other cameras and, with practice, can be nearly as fast to focus as the latest autofocus cameras, but with greater accuracy in low-light situations.

Size and weight are another area in which medium format viewfinder and rangefinder cameras excel. Where most medium format SLRs are sizeable and weighty beasts, rangefinder and viewfinder cameras are significantly smaller, lighter, and easier to use. Some cameras, such as the classic Zeiss Ikonta folding cameras, can provide top-notch results in a camera that will fit in your pocket or take up less room than a 35mm camera body in your camera bag. Even larger models with interchangeable lenses, such as the Mamiya 7, are a little larger than current 35mm professional cameras, such as the Nikon F5.

The final advantage, and perhaps the most important of all, is that the viewfinder or rangefinder design frees lens designers from many of the constraints found in other camera types. In an SLR, for example, designers must ensure the rear element does not protrude into the body and interfere with the camera mirror. Because of the mirror box, some compromises must be made in the optical design. On a viewfinder or rangefinder camera, the lack of mirror means there is no such need to space the lens a certain distance from the film plane, allowing much greater freedom in lens design.

Ansco Titan, 6x6 format, coated 90mm f4.5 Anastigmat lens.

Also, because there is no mirror to cause vibration and degrade image quality, you can get the very best out of the lens at all times. As a result, current rangefinder cameras, not SLRs, have the best lenses in medium format and can provide the highest resolution images. Likewise, because of this optical advantage to the rangefinder design, many well designed, professional rangefinders of yesteryear, such as the Koni-Omega Rapid, can produce images that match the best modern computer-designed SLR lenses.

In all, the rangefinder offers a very complete package that is ideally suited to both general photography and action situations such as weddings. Their quality and reasonable prices make them excellent choices, provided you don't require the ability to cover extreme close-up work, and don't mind the occasional difficulties with rotating-mount filters.

☐ Folding Cameras

Often found in the junk bin at flea markets or antique stores, the folding camera is one of the most overlooked in all of photography. With prices generally ranging from $10 to $75, you can find good quality at very reasonable prices. This also makes medium format, not 35mm, one of the cheapest options to enter serious photography. The reason prices tend to be so cheap is because of the features (or lack thereof) of folding cameras, and also the large number of these cameras available.

Zeiss Ikonta C, 6x9 format, uncoated 105mm lens in Derval ball-bearing shutter with five speeds—$\frac{1}{25}$ second, $\frac{1}{50}$ second, $\frac{1}{100}$ second, B, and T.

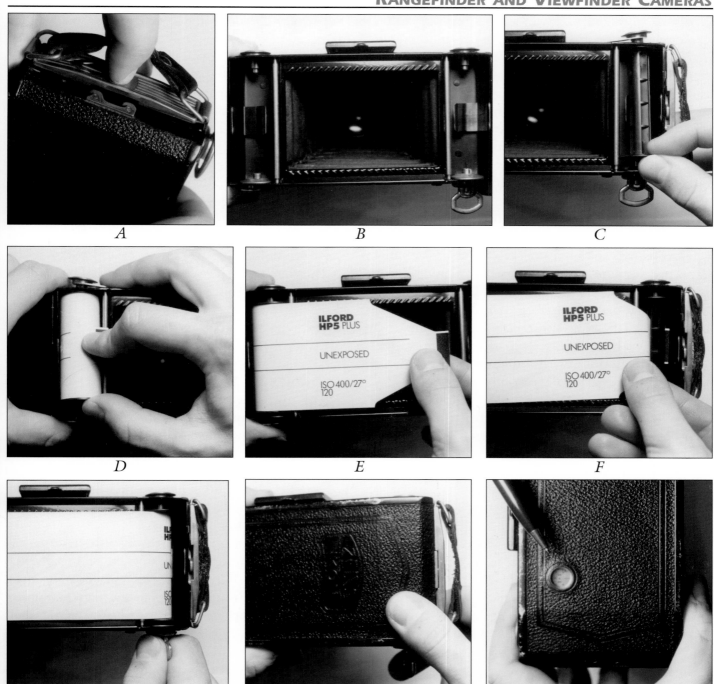

A

B

C

D

E

F

G

H

I

Loading a folding camera. A) Open the back of the camera. B) The inside of the film chamber is incredibly simple, but will vary a bit from camera to camera. With the Zeiss Ikonta used here, the film goes on the left side, and the take-up spool is on the right. The Ansco Titan is the reverse—film on the right, take-up on the left. Just note that the take-up spool goes on the side with the crank, and everything will fall into place. C) Load the take-up spool into the camera. D) Load the film into the camera. With some cameras, you can simply push the film into place as shown. On others, you may need to pull up a knob or pin before you can put in the roll of film. E) Pull the film across the film chamber, making sure the black faces towards the lens and the printed back faces you. F) Insert the leader into the take-up spool. G) Wind the film until it is securely on the spool. H) Close and lock the back. I) Crank the film until you see the red window indicates frame one. As the photo shows, the frame number may not be centered in the window.

Film and Film Advance. In general, folding cameras use the old red-window advance system. Rather than automatically advancing to the next frame as on most cameras, you manually advance the film to the next frame by reading the frame numbers found on the paper backing of 120 film. The red window allows you to read the numbers while minimizing the chances of fogging the film. Later cameras, such as the Zeiss Super Ikonta, have either automatic or semiautomatic film advance, but the vast majority of folding cameras use the red window system. Common film formats are 645, 6x6, and 6x9, offering tremendous freedom of choice.

Exposure. Folding cameras also have very simple exposure systems, and almost never include a light meter. Lenses are mounted in leaf shutters, which must be manually set before each exposure (except on early ball bearing shutters, which automatically reset after each exposure). Focusing is generally done by scale, so shooting with the lens stopped down to f11 or smaller is generally recommended.

Lens. Image quality can be highly variable depending on the camera, but there are a surprising number of solid performers out there. Kodak folding cameras with coated Anastigmat lenses, for example, provide very good image quality and are

exceptional bargains at $10-25 from your local flea market. The Agfa Isolete is another good example, with a lens that provides quite acceptable results in enlargements up to 8"x10", and at $35-50 is another inexpensive option with good quality results. For those willing to spend a bit more, a number of cameras featuring Tessar lenses can be found, and later coated examples such as those found on the Zeiss Ikon cameras will match the image quality found in the Rolleiflex TLRs with Tessar or Xenar lenses. In general, good folding cameras will provide quality enlargements up to 8"x10" or 11"x14". This is particularly true for photographers who use them to shoot in black and white.

Purchasing. When considering a folding camera, make sure everything works before plunking down your hard-earned cash. Many of these cameras cannot be repaired, or simply aren't worth the repair cost if broken. Check the shutter to make sure it works at all speeds, and that the focusing system performs smoothly. Also try to find a model with a coated lens, and at least four elements if possible (open the shutter at B or T and count the reflections—each reflection is a lens element). Coated three-element lenses also work reasonably well, but in any case, make sure the lens is clear and free of fungus or haze. For purely black and white work, older uncoated lenses will work well, particularly if you prefer images with that classic soft-focus look.

In all, the compact size, reasonable performance, and cheap cost make these cameras ideal for trying medium format. For 35mm shooters, they also provide a compact camera to toss in the camera bag for those situations where you want to use a larger negative, but don't want the added size or weight of a fully-featured medium format camera. Finally, for those looking for a compact medium format snapshot camera to carry at all times, look no further than these classic folders.

☐ Box Cameras

There's an old saying in photography: a camera is simply a box with a lens that holds film. Box cameras are the epitome of this sage statement. Since the majority of box cameras that use 120 film are old and have poor lenses, they certainly can't be considered the most serious of photographic tools. However, they offer something that few other cameras can offer—a great deal of fun at virtually no cost.

☐ Keep One on Hand

How many times have you heard someone moan, "If only I had my camera with me, I could have taken the most beautiful picture"? Most of us have missed great pictures simply because we didn't have a camera with us. Classic folding cameras offer a unique opportunity in this regard. Because of their compact size and cheap cost, you can keep one on hand at all times. One photographer I spoke to some time ago owns two folders in addition to his medium format SLR system. One folder lives in his desk at work, and the other is always in his car in case he comes across an interesting photo opportunity. Why? Because he found that many of the best opportunities for pictures come up not when you are out with your complete system intending to take a photograph, but in the moments where your camera is safely locked in the closet at home. Even for those who don't shoot medium format, having a folding camera around can be quite useful for capturing those sudden opportunities with a quality image—thanks to the larger negative size.

When buying a few items at an antique store, the owner tossed in this old Kodak box for free. With a 6"x9" negative and a simple shutter that fires at ¹⁄₂₅ second or so (I think...), the camera makes a good conversation piece and is also fun to occasionally take out just to see what pictures I can get. With a glass lens, you could consider it a step above a Holga, but it still produces very soft images with extremely inexact exposure. (Shown with film insert removed.)

Kodak Brownies and other old, wooden box cameras can be purchased for $10 or less, and generally have shutters with only one speed. In this regard, they are like the Holga and Diana cameras that took the world by storm (although these old boxes generally don't have the same light leak problems as the Holga or Diana). Just as there are a number of people who have fun with the images from those cameras, the old box cameras can also provide hours of amusement and unique images.

The Zeiss Box Tengor, with a coated (!!!) Goertz lens, is capable of producing some decent images. Like the Kodak box, this camera is one that provides much amusement and some interesting images.

☐ Interchangeable Lens Cameras

While folding and box cameras provide excellent options for fun and solid amateur use, stepping up into an interchangeable lens system can expand the possibilities and allow for greater creative freedom. However, there is a general impression that interchangeable lens cameras tend to be expensive, and that the cheaper ones tend to be of lower quality. This is certainly not the case with medium format rangefinder cameras, as less expensive cameras such as the Mamiya Press 23 still produce top-notch performance and remain popular with serious amateurs

and professionals. For those seeking the absolute best quality, cameras such as the Alpa 12wa and the Mamiya rangefinders offer the best modern photography has to offer. In all, medium format interchangeable lens rangefinders offer exceptional value for any budget and should be seriously considered.

Koni-Omega. The Koni-Omega cameras are actually updated versions of the Simmons-Omega cameras produced for the US military in the 1940s and 1950s. Designed as solid professional cameras and built to withstand heavy abuse, the Koni-Omega 6x7 rangefinder cameras are exceptionally reliable with many still in active professional use. For many years, the Koni-Omega was a popular choice with wedding photographers, and these professional tanks remain in active service to this day. Recently, at a close friend's wedding, the photographer used a Koni-Omega with 220 backs to cover the event. In all models, the viewfinder is parallax-corrected and provides split-image focusing. With later models offering interchangeable film backs and lenses still respected for their quality, these cameras offer a tremendous value in medium format with features usually found in cameras costing two to three times as much.

Koni-Omega Bodies. *Koni-Omega Rapid.* The original offering from Konica, the Omega Rapid provides the basis for all later cameras. The viewfinder is parallax compensating, and the shutter on the lens is automatically set when the film is advanced. The interchangeable film magazines make reloading easier, but the back cannot be changed mid-roll, nor are the magazines for this camera compatible with later models. Film is advanced by pulling out a lever on the film back. To ensure proper advance, negative spacing, and shutter cocking, pull the film advance lever out entirely until the counter clicks to the next exposure. After the tenth exposure, the advance bar will lock in the film back. Press the small switch on the film back to unlock it, and then advance until the counter reads *load*. Reload the film back, put the magazine back on the camera, and advance the counter to one to continue shooting.

Koni-Omega Rapid M. An upgrade from the original Rapid, the only major difference is that film magazines are removable in mid-roll, thanks to the addition of a darkslide. This film back is compatible with all later cameras, and has a darkslide holder built into the film insert.

Koni-Omega M. The same camera as the Rapid M, but with a different designation. Both later Rapid M and M models have markings for the 135mm lens, whereas earlier models do not.

Koni-Omega 100. A budget version of the Rapid 200, this camera takes only film inserts, and film cannot be changed mid-roll. The inserts are the same as those used in the Rapid M and 200 magazines. Both Rapid 100 and 200 models have markings for the 135mm lens. Models created for the Japanese market

---

"...neither the name nor focal-length designation denotes a difference in optical design..."

are designated the Konica Press 1.

Koni-Omega Rapid 200. The exact same camera as the Rapid M, but with a new designation to match with the Rapid 100. Models manufactured for the Japanese market were designated the Konica Press 2.

Koni-Omega Lenses. *58mm or 60mm f5.6.* A solid wide-angle lens, it provides rangefinder coupling for focusing, but framing must be done with an external viewfinder. Omegon and Hexanon names were used on the lens, and the lens was marked either 58mm or 60mm depending on when it was manufactured. However, neither the name nor focal-length designation denotes a difference in optical design—they are all the same lenses.

90mm f3.5. The standard lens for the camera, it is available in both Super Omegon and Hexanon designations. Again, name differences between lenses do not denote optical change. All Omegon and Hexanon lenses are optically identical. All lenses have mechanical leaf shutters with speeds from 1 second to $\frac{1}{500}$ second, plus B and full MX sync (with recessed MX switch to prevent accidental change).

135mm: A mild telephoto, this lens was only produced for approximately two years. It is a rare piece, and tends to cost more than any of the other lenses because of the limited production.

180mm f4.5: A well-designed telephoto, this lens is ideal for portraits in 6x7.

Graflex XL. Famous for their Speed Graphic and Crown Graphic cameras, which served as the standard press cameras for many years, Graflex was well versed in creating excellent cameras for serious photography. The XL series is no exception.

Reliable and with a wide assortment of lenses from top manufacturers, the XL series is an excellent rangefinder camera. With the optional Graflok back, a large number of film backs and accessories can be attached to the camera—including a ground glass back. Spacers up to 3¾ inches in length allow for close-up photography, with magnifications as high as 0.5:1 on the XLS or XLRF with 58mm lens. This, combined with the number of excellent lenses available, makes the XL series cameras extremely versatile and suitable for use both in the field and in the studio. The standard film format is 6x7, although other film backs and formats can be used on the camera (including 6x9).

Graflex XL Bodies. *XLS.* The "standard" XL camera, focusing is done by scale or by ground glass. The camera will take all XL lenses and accessories, but is best suited to tripod and ground glass use. The XLS also came in an aerial configuration for use with the 180mm lens, featuring an aerial viewfinder and twin handle grip.

XLRF. The XLRF adds a coupled rangefinder to the XLS, making it the most popular member of the XL series. Like the Koni-Omegas and the Mamiya Press cameras, the XLRF is well suited to general photography and professional applications such as weddings. However, with the Graflok option and ground glass, the XL cameras can be used for close-up work where other rangefinders cannot. For both general photography and technical work, the XLRF serves well.

XLSW. Designed for use with the Schneider 47mm f8 Super Angulon, the XLSW was designed specifically for superwide photography. In terms of features, it matches those of the XLS—a metal body upon which to mount your lens and film holder. In order to use lenses other than the 47mm SA, you need to install a one-inch XL spacer (an extension

Graflex XL camera outfit. Photo courtesy Graflex.

tube that fits on the back of the camera rather than the front). With the spacer installed, the camera is in every respect like the XLS.

Graflex XL Lenses. All lenses feature leaf-shutters, which must be manually set before each exposure. Speeds are one second to ⅟₅₀₀ second plus B (except for the 150mm Ysarex and 100mm Planar which have top speeds of ⅟₄₀₀ second). Available lenses are as follows: 47mm f8 Schneider Super Angulon (XLSW only); 58mm f5.6 Rodenstock Grandagon; 80mm f2.8 Noritar (budget lens); 80mm f2.8 Zeiss Planar; 95mm f2.8 Rodenstock Heligon; 95mm f3.5 Rodenstock Ysarex; 100mm f3.5 Noritar (full coverage for 3¼"x4¼" Polaroids); 100mm f3.5 Zeiss Tessar; 100mm f2.8 Zeiss Planar; 150mm f4.5 Rodenstock Ysarex; 180mm f4.5 Rodenstock Rotelar; 180mm f4.8 Zeiss Sonnar, and 270mm f6.6 Rodenstock Roletar.

Mamiya Press 23. Like the Koni-Omega and Graflex XL cameras, the Mamiya Press cameras have maintained a loyal following. In fact, the Mamiya Universal Press remained in production until 1991, a testament to the quality and popularity of the design. Of all the older press and rangefinder cameras, the Mamiya is perhaps the most versatile system, because there exists not only a wide range of lenses and film backs, but also the provision for tilt and swing on the rear standard, allowing for limited perspective control and also making the camera useful for close-up photography. All bodies feature coupled rangefinders compatible with all lenses in the system, with automatic parallax compensation available in later models. While the camera was designed as a 6x9 format camera, 6x7 backs tend to be more readily available, and the majority of Mamiya Press cameras that I have seen for sale include 6x7 backs rather than the 6x9.

Mamiya Press 23 Bodies. *Mamiya Press Deluxe.* The original Press camera, it offers a coupled rangefinder, rear tilt and swing, and compatibility with all Mamiya backs.

Mamiya Press G. Functionally the same as the Press Deluxe, the G features a Graflok back rather than a Mamiya back. All Graflok compatible accessories, including film backs and ground glass adaptors, will fit this camera.

Mamiya Press S. An economy version of the Press Deluxe, this camera features a fixed 105mm lens and lacks the rear movements found on the Press.

Mamiya Press Standard. The Standard is the same as the S, except with lens interchangeability added.

Mamiya Press Super 23. A significant upgrade over the Standard, the Super 23 offers auto parallax compensation and also provides the rear movements found on the original Press Deluxe. This camera accepts sheet film holders and all Mamiya backs.

Mamiya Universal Press. Introduced in 1969, the Universal offers all the features of the Super 23, but takes both Mamiya and Graflok backs and accessories. Instead of mounting a film back directly onto the camera, you first mount a back adaptor onto the camera, and then the film back onto the adaptor (M adaptor for Mamiya backs and G adaptor for Graflok accessories). The Universal also has a switch in the viewfinder to change framing from 6x9 to 6x7, and also to adjust for the 100mm, 150mm, and 250mm lenses. The Universal also features a reinforced lens mount to handle the weight of the 250mm lens. Of all the Press bodies, the Universal is by far the most advanced and most desirable.

Mamiya Universal Press Lenses. These lenses include: 50mm f6.3, 75mm f5.6, 90mm, 100mm f2.8, 100mm f3.5, 127mm f4.7, 150mm f5.6, 250mm f5. All lenses feature leaf shutters that must be set before exposure. As with the Mamiya TLR cameras, earlier lenses will be chrome, while later lenses will be black.

Alpa. Handmade in Switzerland with the same precision found in fine Swiss watches, the Alpa represents a unique and exceptional quality product which is a testament to the company's enduring legacy in the photographic world. This is a camera designed and produced for serious photography, but with close attention also paid to the aesthetics.

The Alpa 12 system. Photo courtesy of Alpa.

The Alpa 12 and PhaseOne's LightPhase digital back. Photo courtesy of PhaseOne and Alpa.

Aside from the excellent construction and beauty of this fine photographic machine, Alpa offers an impressive range of lenses. While available lenses include the 35mm Rodenstock Grandagon and the tremendous optics of the Schneider 47mm and 58mm Super-Angulon XL, Alpa offers the world a first—the amazing 38mm Zeiss Biogon in an interchangeable lens mount. For many, the ability to use the Schneider 47mm Super Angulon XL and the Zeiss Biogon on the same camera provides strong incentives to purchase the Alpa, but the desirability of this camera extends well beyond the lenses it takes.

The Alpa 12 comes in two versions: the 12wa, and the 12s/wa. Both are viewfinder cameras, with focusing either done by the scale on the lens' helicoid mount or by using a ground glass. The 12s/wa provides the user with 25mm of shift capability, which is particularly useful for landscapes and architectural photography, where the 12wa is a standard rigid body with no movements.

Aside from the precision of the camera body and available optics, Alpa has made available a wide range of accessories and film backs for the camera. Film backs include modified Mamiya RB-67 film backs, Linhof Cine Rollex backs, and Linhof Super Rollex backs in formats ranging from the unique 66mm x 44mm through 6x9, with virtually every format in between also available. Many film backs from other medium format systems can also be used with back adaptors. Digital and Polaroid backs can also be used with the camera, rounding out an already impressive set of available film backs and ensuring useful life in the digital world.

With the wide assortment of accessories and top notch optics, Alpa should be on your short list if you are a fan of wide angle photography or precision photographic tools. With Schneider Optics now distributing the cameras in the U.S., these fine cameras should become much more readily available.

Alpa Lenses. Available lenses include: *Rodenstock (including helical mount) Copal 0 (manual cocking; B, T, 1/500-1s)*
- Apo-Grandagon 4.5/35mm
- Apo-Grandagon 4.5/45mm
- Apo-Grandagon 4.5/55mm
- 65, 75, 100, 135, 150mm and self-cocking shutters on request

Schneider (including helical mount) Copal 0 (manual cocking; B, T, 1/500-1s)
- Super-Angulon XL 5.6/47mm
- Super-Angulon XL 5.6/58mm
- 65, 75, 100, 120, 135, 150mm and self-cocking shutters on request

Zeiss (including helical mount) Compur 0 (manual cocking; B, 1/500-1s)
- Biogon T* 4.5/38mm

Fuji. Fuji currently produces a line of excellent fixed-lens rangefinder cameras in a variety of film formats, including 645, 6x7, and 6x9. These cameras have been popular since they first hit the market due to their extremely reasonable size and weight, in addition to top-notch optics. The 6x9 cameras, in particular, stand out in the size and weight areas. While certainly not the smallest of cameras, the Fuji 6x9s are very easy to carry and use in the field and offer weight significantly less than some medium format SLR cameras.

Of all the Fuji rangefinders, the most noteworthy is the Fuji 645Zi—the only true "point-and-shoot" camera in medium format with a 55–90mm zoom lens, autofocus, automatic exposure, built-in flash, and even automatic film advance with data imprinting available! However, unlike 35mm point and shoot cameras, where optics tend to be less than stellar, the zoom on the Fuji 645Zi is truly top notch and capable of excellent, professional-quality results. This has made it an exceptional medium format travel camera, and a popular snapshot camera used by wedding photographers at receptions for medium format quality with point-and-shoot ease of use. Likewise, the 645Wi offers the same ease of use and portability as the 645Zi, but with a fixed 45mm f4 lens instead of the 55–90mm zoom, and the 645i offers a 60mm lens.

All in all, the Fuji rangefinders (including all current and past models) are deserving of serious consideration if you are looking for a professional quality camera that is more portable and easier to use in the field than an SLR camera—provided you don't mind the fixed lens rangefinder design.

Current models are: GA-645I with 60mm f4 lens, GA-645Wi with 45mm f4 lens, GA-645Zi with 55–90mm lens, GW-6x7 with 90mm f3.5 lens, GSW-6x9 with 65mm f5.6 wide-angle lens, and GW-6x9 with 90mm f3.5 standard lens.

Mamiya 6 and 7 Rangefinder Cameras. For those demanding the best lenses in medium format, the answer is not Zeiss, as many think. The crown for best lenses in medium format belongs to the Mamiya rangefinders, with an honorable mention to the Zeiss Planar found on the latest Rollei TLR cameras. Because of the lack of mirror box and similar design constraints common with SLR lens design, Mamiya was able to create lenses with few compromises for their rangefinder cameras. As a result, the Mamiya lenses have been recognized as the best in medium format—by both photographers and independent tests.

> *"The crown for best lenses in medium format belongs to the Mamiya rangefinders..."*

When you consider the fact that their size and weight is little more than a Nikon F5 with lens, these cameras make ideal field cameras, especially for wedding photography and similar action uses. With their excellent lens selection, the Mamiya rangefinders can also be used for landscapes or portraiture with little difficulty. However, it should be noted that the Mamiyas are not well-suited to close-up work or the studio. For field use, on the other hand, the Mamiya rangefinders are among the very best available, with their size and weight being very similar to current professional 35mm cameras.

Mamiya 6. Introduced in 1989, the Mamiya 6 was the first of the new Mamiya rangefinders to be produced. Offering exceptional lenses and a 6x6 negative, the camera quickly gained a strong group of advocates. The camera offers a built-in meter with autoexposure, and focusing is done by split-image rangefinder with parallax compensation. Available lenses are 50mm f4, 75mm f3.5, and 150mm f4.5.

Mamiya 6MF. The 6MF takes the solid design of the 6, and then adds multi-format capability (hence the MF designation). With the 645 kit installed, the 6MF is capable of making twelve 56mm x 44mm images on 120 film (24 on 220) in vertical format. This format corresponds exactly to the aspect ratio of an 8"x10" print, allowing for the entire negative to be used when printing. The 6MF also offers 24mm x 56mm panoramic images on 35mm film, rounding out its multi-format capabilities.

"For under $50, you can find a folding camera with an old reflective meter..."

Mamiya 7. Following the success of the 6 series, Mamiya introduced the Mamiya 7 with a negative size of 6x7. With electronically timed leaf-shutters in lens, the 7 offers flash sync at all speeds, from four seconds to $\frac{1}{500}$ second. Like the 6, the 7 offers aperture priority autoexposure and a split image rangefinder with parallax compensating viewfinder. Like the 6MF, the 7 offers a panoramic adaptor for 35mm film, but in the popular 24mm x 65mm for-mat (1:2.7 aspect ratio). Available lenses for the camera are a 43mm f4.5 (separate finder required for framing), 50mm f4.5 (separate finder required for framing), 65mm f4, 80mm f4, and 150mm f4.5. Mamiya 6 lenses are not compatible with the 7, nor are 7 lenses compatible with the 6.

Mamiya 7-II. Introduced with the 50mm f4.5, the Mamiya 7-II builds on the original 7 by adding a brighter viewfinder and multiple exposure capability. In all, a truly excellent camera well worth consider-ing if your budget can accomodate it.

☐ Conclusion

With many excellent options to consider in a variety of price ranges, rangefinder and viewfinder cameras deserve serious consideration—par-ticularly for those simply interested in trying medium format at low cost. For under $50, you can find a folding camera with an old reflective meter such as a Weston Master, and be ready to go. For those who require profes-sional quality results, many of the older rangefinders can provide top-notch performance at very low cost. The latest rangefinders, including lesser known cam-eras such as the Plaubel Makina, offer performance that will exceed that of the best modern SLRs. In all, rangefinders offer one of the best options for field use, with their relatively compact size, reasonable weight, and excellent handling.

Chapter 5

The Single Lens Reflex

Of all camera types, none is more closely associated with serious photography than the SLR. Its greatest advantage is the ability to allow the photographer to view through the same lens used to take the photograph, thus giving the ability to more precisely frame images. This ability to show the photographer exactly what will appear on film offers a tremendous advantage. SLRs also offer the best lens selection. Even older SLR systems offer at least five to six lens options, and some modern SLR systems offer twenty or more lenses including fixed, zoom, and special purpose lenses.

☐ Mirror

Given this, many people consider the SLR the most versatile and capable of all cameras—yet certain drawbacks must be kept in mind. One of the largest disadvantages of an SLR is the mirror itself. While allowing the photographer to view through the taking lens, the mirror introduces a number of significant problems. The first problem with medium format SLRs is physical size. Because the mirror is relatively large, the camera body itself becomes sizeable, and with lens and film back, a medium format SLR can become quite large and heavy, particularly in the case of 6x7 SLR cameras.

When handling a medium format SLR, fire the shutter and you will feel the vibration from the mirror. Unlike in dancing, if you feel the vibration here, it's not a good thing—vibration in the camera due to mirror slap can noticeably reduce sharpness, even at higher shutter speeds. Because of mirror vibration on most medium format SLRs, shutter speeds $\frac{1}{30}$ second and slower should not be used without mirror lockup. With some 6x7 SLRs (the Pentax 6x7 in particular), the mirror slap is signifi-

cant enough that mirror lockup is recommended at all speeds.

The SLR's mirror also presents a problem for lens designers. Because of the mirror, rear elements can not protrude into the camera body itself without blocking the mirror travel. This means that the lens must sit a certain distance away from the film plane, which makes designing lenses much more difficult—particularly in the case of wide angle lenses. As a result, SLR lenses require more complicated and expensive designs to produce quality images, and even after such extensive design, an SLR lens may not be able to match the quality of an unrestricted design such as those produced for current rangefinders, TLRs, or large format.

> ## "...fire the shutter and you will feel the vibration from the mirror."

That being said, modern SLR lenses are still capable of top-notch performance, thanks in part to advanced computer design. Keep in mind that current SLR lenses are built to professional standards, which means that a modern SLR lens will perform far better than earlier lenses found on cameras of any type. And, while current unrestricted designs such as those for the Mamiya 7 are technically better than current SLR lenses, modern SLR lenses are capable of exceptional images and perform well under even the most technical demands.

☐ Viewfinder

Another area of the SLR often overlooked is the viewfinder itself. While people often assume that what you see on the focusing screen is exactly what

As with a TLR camera, make sure to support the camera from underneath when shooting.

will appear on film, this is rarely the case. Few SLR viewfinders truly offer 100% coverage, with most giving 90–95% coverage. This means that, while what you see in the viewfinder will be caught on film, there is an additional 5–10% that you don't see that will also appear on film. Thus, the popular SLR battle cry "What you see is what you get!" is not in complete agreement with reality.

☐ Film Backs

One area in which medium format SLRs often outdo their TLR and rangefinder counterparts is in the area of film backs. With a number of modern SLR cameras such as those from Hasselblad, interchangeable film backs are standard equipment. Provided you don't lose your darkslide, you can change film in mid-roll, allowing you to shoot both black and white and color at the same time without a second camera

body—or reload on the fly by simply putting a fresh film back on the camera. Even if film backs are not interchangeable, cameras such as the Pentax 645 use film inserts to make loading faster and easier.

☐ Finders and Accessories

Modern SLR cameras also tend to offer the widest range of finders and accessories. Bronica, for example, has one of the most modular systems on the market, and currently offers six different finders for the ETR series cameras. Bellows attachments, interchangeable focusing screens, and different winders are all standard options on the majority of current medium format SLRs, bolstering their position as the most versatile of all medium format cameras.

Despite the drawbacks caused by the mirror, the SLR remains the most popular and versatile choice. With the wide range of lenses and accessories, an SLR can be used for virtually any type of photography and is limited only by the size and weight of the equipment. 645 and 6x6 SLRs are particularly well-suited to both field and studio work as they are reasonable in size and weight. With accessory grips, they can be handled nearly as easily as a 35mm camera.

In the end, the most significant drawback to most photographers looking at medium format SLR systems is cost. Even the oldest SLR cameras tend to cost $300-400 or more for a complete camera. A modern SLR camera body can cost over $1000 new.

☐ "Classic" SLR Cameras

For those who want an SLR, but can't afford a current model, classic SLR cameras offer a tremendous value. You can often buy a complete camera for a fraction of the cost of a current model, and buy additional lenses at relatively low cost. It is not uncommon to find cameras such as the Bronica S2A complete with lens and film back for $350–450. Additional lenses cost only $150–350, in most cases. Compare this to a current Bronica system, and the savings is obvious.

However, the reference to these cameras as "classic" or "old" doesn't always hold. Kowa, for example, continued to produce their cameras well into the early 1980s, so many are no older than Hasselblad 500 C/M bodies still in professional use today. The reference to these cameras as "classics" means simply that the cameras are no longer produced or widely supported, and are incompatible with current SLR systems. In the case of Kowa and Graflex, neither company exists any longer as a manufacturer of medium format equipment, relegating all their cameras to the classics category.

The main drawback to the classic SLR is in reliability and ease of repair. Because many of the classic SLR cameras are significantly older than their more modern cousins, the chances of mechanical failure are greater. Should a classic SLR need repairs, parts and service become an issue. Parts are generally more difficult to find, and often must be harvested from another broken camera. Even if you have the parts (or can find them), a repairman capable of fixing the camera may not be easy to find with certain cameras—as one repairman I spoke with commented, in regards to the Norita 66, that few people know how to repair the cameras. However, the lenses for the Norita and other classic SLR cameras are generally well regarded, particularly the Nikkor lenses for the early Bronica cameras.

"With a little machining, lenses can be easily adapted to the camera..."

Classic SLRs are particularly well-suited to amateur use, where the volume of shooting is limited. Professionals and high-volume shooters may wish to consider a classic SLR as a backup camera, but should not use them as their main medium format camera. In looking at a classic SLR, condition is extremely important; make sure any classic SLR you select is in good working order, and is in excellent cosmetic condition. The better the condition, the less likely you are to have difficulties down the road. In all, classic SLRs offer excellent options for amateurs looking for an SLR on a budget.

Early Bronica. Of all classic SLRs, the early Bronica cameras are the most often referenced in conversation. Designed to complete against Hasselblad, the Bronicas earned a reputation as "the poor man's Hasselblad," although it is still unclear if the nickname was meant in respect or contempt of the cameras. What is certainly very clear is that the Nikkor lenses designed for the camera are truly excellent, and still are considered capable of producing professional-quality results. When you consider

that many of these lenses can be found for $150–250, they are undeniable bargains in medium format. The camera bodies, on the other hand, don't share such a solid reputation.

As some professional photographers have commented, owning one of the early Bronicas is like owning a Jaguar. You actually needed to have two—one to use while the other is in the repair shop. Many photographers found that, under professional use, the cameras simply did not hold up as well as other cameras (such as Rolleiflex and Hasselblad). However, because the cameras were relatively inexpensive and the lenses were impressive, the early Bronicas garnered a solid following, and many are still in use by amateurs today. Bronica also earned a reputation as an innovator, introducing a number of firsts in medium format SLRs, such as electronically controlled shutter speeds with the Bronica EC in March 1972.

Because the focusing helical is built into the camera, the early Bronica SLRs have become popular with tinkerers. With a little machining, lenses can be easily adapted to the camera, including 35mm lenses or view camera lenses. Bronica even made a "blank mount adaptor" for the Bronica Deluxe and S models. This could be machined to accept press lenses, helping set the precedent for adapting lenses to the cameras.

For current photographers, the early Bronicas are perfect for amateurs on a budget who want access to a wide range of quality optics, but cannot afford a current SLR model. The primary difficulty with the early Bronica cameras tends to be soft advance gearing. Under rough or heavy usage, these gears can strip, causing uneven spacing or an inability to advance the film (in the worst case scenario). On most models, advance is done by a knob with a fold-out crank. To prevent stripping, Bronica owners highly recommend not using the crank and advancing by use of the knob only. If this precaution is followed, Bronicas in good condition can be reliable—provided they are not subjected to extremely heavy or rough usage.

Early Bronica Bodies. *Bronica Deluxe (or "D").* The first Bronica SLR, it features a focal plane shutter with speeds up to $\frac{1}{1250}$ second—one of the fastest in medium format, both current and past. The camera also features a variable self timer, which can be set

Bronica EC-TL. Photo courtesy of Bronica.

from two to ten seconds, and also acts as a timed long exposure—another feature not often seen in medium format. It takes all small bayonet lenses and interchangeable backs (Deluxe backs only).

Bronica S. A simplified version of the Deluxe, its shutter tops out at 1/1000 second and the self timer, double exposure control, and focus lock were all eliminated. It will take all small bayonet lenses, and

can take the tele-Nikkor lenses with a special focusing adaptor. The 105mm f3.5 Nikkor and 300mm f4.5 Zenzanon will not fit this camera. The camera also requires special extension tubes and bellows for close-up work. This camera accepts all S and S2 series film backs. Mirror lock is available by a switch below the shutter release. All prisms, hoods, and grips for the S and later S2 cameras will fit.

Bronica C. An economy version of the S, the C lacks interchangeable backs. It takes the same film inserts as the S2/S2A film backs, and will take all lenses and accessories. A special adaptor allows the use of the original model S bellows on the C and later models. This is the only early Bronica without interchangeable film backs.

Bronica S2. An updated version of the S, it features a removable focusing helical, and can be found in black or chrome.

Bronica S2A. The gem of the classic Bronica line, the S2A is an internally modified version of the S2. The modifications were actually improvements to the advance mechanism, making the S2A a very reliable camera. However, with a flash sync speed of only $\frac{1}{40}$ second and a loud mirror flop, the S2A is best used for general photography and situations where the mirror thump won't be disturbing. Identified by the S2A designation after the serial number, or with serial numbers of 150037 and higher.

Bronica EC. With electronically controlled shutter speeds from four seconds to $\frac{1}{1000}$ second, the EC represented a new generation of cameras for Bronica. Mirror lockup, a locking PC terminal, and interchangeable focusing screens can also be found on the camera. All lenses fit the camera, but the EC will only take EC finders and film backs.

"The body itself is rather distinctive in that it is similar in size to a TLR camera..."

Bronica EC-TL. The EC-TL offers aperture priority autoexposure, one of the first medium format cameras to do so. The EC-TL metering will even work with the waist-level finder, another rarity in medium format SLRs. It takes all EC finders and backs, and all lenses except for the 105mm f3.5 Nikkor.

Early Bronica Lenses.
Small Bayonet
- Nikkor: 40mm f4, 50mm f3.5, 50mm f2.8, 75mm f2.8 (HC and PC versions), 135mm f3.5, 200mm f4 (older versions will have focal length in centimeters)
- Zenzanon: 40mm f4, 50mm f2.8, 75mm f2.8, 80mm f2.8, 80mm f2.4, 100mm f2.8,

150mm f3.5, 200mm f3.5 (some Zenzanon lenses were designed by Carl Zeiss Jena—such as the 80mm f2.8)

Large Bayonet
- Nikkor: 105mm f3.5 (leaf shutter), 300mm f5.6, 400mm f4.5, 600mm f5.6, 800mm f8, 1200mm f11. 400mm and higher telephotos require focusing mount #81505 for proper mounting and use on the camera.
- Zenzanon: 300mm f4.5

Nikon Adapter
- An often confused item, this allows Nikon short mount telephoto lenses for the RF camera (180mm, 250mm, 350mm, 500mm) to be used on the Deluxe and S models, and is only compatible with these cameras.

Other Lenses
- A number of off-brand lenses were made to fit the Bronica cameras, making lenses even more readily available for the camera. Komura, for example, made a full line of lenses to fit Bronica cameras.

Kowa. Another camera sometimes referred to as a "poor man's Hasselblad," the Kowa cameras were in production through the early 1980s. All lenses are of modern design and are fully coated, and thus perform quite well. The body itself is rather distinctive in that it is similar in size to a TLR camera and uses a similar method of film advance. Rather than a insert system like that found on most SLRs, the Kowa uses a vertical advance. This makes the body tall in comparison to other SLRs, but the vertical design does not particularly save on weight, compared to standard SLRs with film backs or inserts.

Like the early Bronica cameras, the first Kowa models have soft advance systems that can be stripped with rough or heavy use. Thus, winding with the knob is recommended (rather than using the crank). The Kowa 66 with interchangeable backs has a much more reliable advance mechanism, but tends to be harder to have fixed if it breaks. Also, like the early Bronicas, the lenses available for the Kowa cameras are sharp and well designed. For fisheye buffs, the Kowa offers a 19mm fisheye lens, a rare and intriguing lens.

I own a Kowa Six with 85mm lens and have been impressed with the quality images from the

Kowa Six. Rarer black body, with black 85mm f2.8 lens.

camera. It definitely deserves serious consideration by those looking for a good medium format SLR at reasonable cost—particularly considering the range of good lenses and finders (both metered and non-metered). However, like the Bronicas, Kowas should not be used by those with extremely heavy shooting requirements, except possibly as a backup camera. For amateur use, the Kowas work very well and a number of photographers still swear by them—particularly when you consider the very reasonable cost of additional lenses.

Kowa Bodies. *Kowa Six.* The original Kowa, the Six is a good basic camera. Finders and focusing screens are interchangeable, and both 120 and 220 film can be used in the camera. All lenses have leaf shutters and speeds from one second to $\frac{1}{500}$ second plus T, with MXV sync and depth of field preview lever. Advance is with a knob (with fold-out crank) on the right side of the camera. The shutter release can be locked to prevent accidental

exposure. Some later bodies can be found painted all black, but most have chrome trim.

Kowa 6MM. All the features of the original Kowa Six, plus multiple exposures and mirror lock up.

Kowa Super 66. Same as the 6MM, but with interchangeable film backs. Of all the Kowa cameras, the Super 66 is by far the most reliable and the best option. The only complaint against the Super 66 is that it can be difficult to remove the film back when the camera is mounted on a tripod.

Kowa Lenses. Available lenses are: 19mm fish-eye, 35mm f4.5, 40mm f4, 55 f3.5, 85mm f2.8, 150mm f3.5, 200mm f4.5, 250mm f5.6. Earlier models are chrome, and later models are black. Extension tubes are available for close-up work.

Norita 66. A rarely seen camera, the Norita 66 is an interesting medium format SLR. Given its size and looks, it could easily be mistaken for a large 35mm SLR. The body itself is barely larger than my Canon Eos A2, making it a very manageable camera. However, it is a full 6x6 SLR, and the large prism and hefty lenses are dead giveaways of a medium for-mat camera. With an impressive array of lenses from 40mm though 400mm, it may seem a bit strange that more of these cameras aren't seen.

Should you come across a Norita in good work-ing order and at a reasonable price, it may be a camera to consider. The lenses are said to be quite good, and the camera can produce fine images while taking up little more room in your bag than a 35mm camera. However, keep in mind that repair service is difficult to find for these cameras, and locating additional lenses and accessories can be problematic.

The body itself offers speeds from one second to $\frac{1}{500}$ second plus B, with X sync at $\frac{1}{40}$ second on a spe-cial X setting on the shutter speed dial. The camera can take either 120 or 220 film without additional accessories or modification. Finders are interchange-able, with the option of a pentaprism, metered TTL prism, or waist-level finder. A right angle finder and two microscope attachments (one with Copal shut-ter) are also available and screens are interchange-able. A very interesting camera, and one well worth considering if you are on a budget.

Norita 66 Lenses. Available lenses are: 40mm f4, 55mm f4, 70mm f3.5 leaf-shutter, 80mm f2.0 (!), 160mm f4, 240mm f4, 400mm f4.5. All lenses offer depth of field preview.

The body of the Norita 66 is barely larger than my Canon Eos A2, making it a very manageable camera. Photo courtesy of Norita.

☐ Current SLR Systems

For those seeking the latest in camera technology, or the most current computer designed lenses, the current SLRs will undoubtedly satisfy. With features such as autofocus and complex autoexposure systems becoming standard features on many cameras (particularly 645s), these cameras are worth the added expense over used equipment. However, for those looking for completely mechanical equipment, cameras such as the Hasselblad 501 CM and the Mamiya RB67 can be easily found.

As with the "classic" label put on the older SLR cameras, "current" also tends to be a bit misleading. With a number of current systems, such as the Bronica ETR or Hasselblad 500 series, older camera bodies are still available that will take the latest lenses and accessories, blurring the line between current and past models. Certainly, the latest cameras have the most advances, but older bodies can certainly be considered current, or at least only a step behind current models. For those looking to enter into a current system but without sufficient funds to spend on a brand-new body, the older cameras will allow you to enter a given system at reduced cost. Additionally, the older cameras often make excellent backup cameras. Thus, when looking at a current system, also consider the older, discontinued models either as backups or comparatively inexpensive options to enter a modern system.

Bronica. Current Bronica cameras represent some of the most modular systems in medium format today, with perhaps the widest range of available

☐ Mirror Lockup

One item that often confuses people on the Bronicas is the mirror lockup system on the current cameras. If operated incorrectly, you can waste frames and get somewhat frustrated with the camera. Here's how to avoid problems. First compose and focus your photograph, then flip the mirror lockup switch to prefire the mirror. Hit the shutter release and take the photo. Before advancing the film, return the lockup switch to its normal position. If you don't, when you advance the film, the shutter will fire and blow out the next frame. After returning the switch to its normal position, advance the film normally.

finders and film backs. All lenses currently available are computer designed, and image quality is among the best in medium format today. Bronica produces SLR cameras in the 645, 6x6, and 6x7 format. In fact, Bronica is one of only two manufacturers currently producing cameras in all three of these most popular formats (the other is Mamiya with the 6MF rangefinder as their sole 6x6 offering). Despite this, while the ETR series cameras are extremely popular with wedding photographers, the Bronica systems tend to be the most overlooked of all the current SLR cameras. While East and West Coast dealers often stock Bronica, Midwest stores generally don't carry the brand.

In truth, I find myself somewhat puzzled as to why the Bronica SLR systems are overlooked, particularly when you look at the features offered by the cameras. The GS-1, for example, is one of the few 6x7 SLR cameras that can truly be considered a good field camera—with size and weight only slightly greater than a 6x6 SLR. The 135-W panoramic backs available for the SQ and ETR series cameras represent the only true interchangeable panoramic backs in medium format today, with an image format of 24mm x 54mm on 35mm film. Mamiya offers a panoramic option for their 645 cameras, but it is a 13mm x 36mm format (like that found in many of today's point-and-shoots), not a true full-frame panoramic. Additionally, the modular nature of the systems, with a wide range of finders, backs, and accessories, makes the cameras extremely versatile. One unique winder is the Speed Grip, which gives a comfortable grip handle with 35mm SLR-style lever advance. With Speed Grip in place, I find my ETRSi handles like an oversized 35mm camera and is very comfortable.

One feature common to all current Bronica systems is an electronically controlled leaf-shutter in the lens. This allows for exceptionally accurate exposures, while also providing flash sync at all speeds. TTL/OTF (Through The Lens/Off The Film) flashmetering is also available in all current systems, by way of the SCA-386 TTL adaptor. This connects directly to Metz flashes with SCA-300 connections.

For both professional and amateur use, the Bronica systems offer exceptionally good value with a range of accessories and features that should satisfy the demands of most photographers. And with automatic exposure prisms available at extremely reasonable cost by medium format standards, Bronica cameras can also be some of the easiest to use.

Bronica ETR Bodies. Of all current Bronica systems, the ETR series cameras are undeniably the most popular. Wedding photographers in particular like the cameras for the additional exposures provided by the 645 format, and also because of the leaf-shutter lenses. Accessories such as the Speed Grip and AE prisms also make the ETR cameras among the easiest handling of the current medium format SLRs. For both studio and field use in 645 format, the ETR cameras are among the very best.

"...Bronica systems offer exceptionally good value with a range of accessories..."

ETR. The ETR series camera was introduced in 1976. The model features an electronically controlled leaf-shutter, and eight second to $\frac{1}{500}$ second shutter speeds with the T setting on the lens. It accepts all ETR backs, lenses, and finders, but does not have automatic exposure with the AE-III finder (all metering functions will work). Multiple exposures are achieved by means of a switch on the right side of the camera above the wind crank.

ETRC. Much like the ETR, but because it uses only film inserts instead of interchangeable backs you are limited to 120 or 220 film with this model.

ETRS. Essentially the same as the ETR, but two features are added. First, it has an additional electronic contact in the viewfinder to allow the meter-

A

B

C

D

E

F

G

H

I

J

K

(Opposite) Loading a medium format SLR camera. A) Open the film back. B) Remove the film insert and put the back off to one side. C) Remove the old film spool from the back—this will be your take-up spool. D) Insert the take-up spool into the proper position (on most 645 and 6x6 cameras, the spool will go onto the bottom position). E) Insert the new roll of film. F) Pull the film up and over the rollers, making sure the black part faces the front towards where the lens will be. G) Insert the leader into the take-up spool. H) Wind the leader onto the take-up spool. I) Stop winding when the arrows on the new roll of film meet the red arrow or dot inside the film chamber. J) Reassemble the film back. K) You're set to go. Note: I used a Bronica ETR film back in this photo set. Backs from Hasselblad, Mamiya, and others will vary in how they open, but the principles of loading them will be the same. The main item to remember is that the black side of the film backing must face the lens once the back is loaded.

ing display on the AE-II and AE-III finders to be lit when the shutter button is depressed slightly (unlike the original AE prism on which you had to press a button on the front of the prism to activate the display). The ETRS also adds a two-position shutter release lock—locked, front release locked (for use with speed grip or motor winder), and all releases unlocked. The ETRS is found in two versions: the early metal version with locking front lens release and the later "plastic" ETRS with the lens release on the left side of the camera. Users have found that the later plastic-bodied ETRS tends to have a rough advance that needs routine maintenance, so the early metal version is preferred.

ETR-C. This camera has all the features of the ETRS, but lacks interchangeable film backs. Essentially, it is an updated version of the ETRC.

ETRSi. The ETRSi incorporates a number of advances over previous models, most notably mirror lockup and TTL flashmetering. A warning flag in the viewfinder when using multiple exposures was also added, and a Bulb shutter setting was added. In addi-

The Bronica ETRSi incorporates advances over previous models, most notably mirror lockup and TTL flashmetering. Photo courtesy of Bronica.

tion, the advance mechanism was redesigned and greatly improved.

Bronica ETR Lenses. Lenses for the ETR series cameras will work on any body with full functionality, allowing you to use the latest PE lens on the earliest ETR body with no difficulties. All lenses feature electronically controlled leaf shutters with speeds from eight seconds to 1/500 second. The earliest series of lenses were designated MC, and for the most part they are very good performers. Two lenses to avoid in the MC line are the 150mm f4 MC and the 75 f2.8 MC—the 150mm f4 because it is a poor performer, and the 75mm because of mediocre performance and a 58mm filter thread (virtually every other ETR lens has a 62mm filter thread). The 150mm f3.5 MC, which replaced the f4 lens, is a true standout, with quality that matches the latest PE version. The MC and E or E-II lenses are optically the same, except for the 75mm f2.8 E-II which is a vast improvement over the MC version. MC and E/E-II lenses offer aperture adjustment only in full stops, where the current PE lenses provide adjustments in two-stop increments. All PE lenses are computer designed.

Fixed Lenses. Fixed lenses include: 30mm f3.5 fisheye, 40mm f4, 50mm f2.8, 60mm f2.8, 75mm f2.8, 100mm f4 Macro (no longer in production), 105mm f4 1:1 Macro, 135mm f4, 150mm f3.5, 150mm f4 (MC only), 180mm f4.5, 200mm f4.5, 250mm f5.6, 500mm f8 (PE version has ED glass).

Special Purpose and Zoom. These lenses include: 45–90mm f4–5.6 PE, 100–220mm f4.8 PE, 2x and 1.4x teleconverters, 55mm f4.5 PE Super Angulon Tilt/Shift (no longer in production), and the Schneider Variogon PE (no longer in production).

Bronica SQ Bodies. For those looking for an alternative to Hasselblad in 6x6 SLRs, Bronica offers the excellent SQ series cameras. With their reasonable size and leaf shutters, the SQ cameras work very well both in the field and in the studio. Additionally, the SQ cameras offer the least expensive AE control in 6x6 SLRs, and lenses that are top-notch but significantly less in price than their Hasselblad or Rollei counterparts. These options, combined with an excellent set of finders and film backs, makes the Bronica SQ cameras worth serious consideration for photographers looking into 6x6—particularly for those on a budget.

SQ. The first SQ series body, it is compatible with all later lenses. However, it will not take later AE prisms, and will only meter with the manual ME prism.

SQ-A. An update of the SQ, the SQ-A adds mirror lockup and a ten-pin contact array in the viewfinder for use with the AE prisms. It will take all SQ accessories and finders, but will not accept the new SQ-i motor drive.

SQ-Am. Bronica introduced the SQ-Am for those who wanted the features of the SQ-A, but also required motorized film advance. Aside from the motor drive (which is integrated into the camera and cannot be removed), the SQ-Am is the same as the SQ-A.

SQ-Ai. The current top model in the SQ series, the SQ-Ai brings a number of updates to the SQ-A. First and foremost is the addition of TTL flashmetering and the modification of the wind crank to take the SQ-i new motor drive. It also features a sixteen-second shutter speed, Bulb setting, and multiple exposure warning flag in the viewfinder. To accept the new motor drive, the wind crank was modified, and SQ-A cranks will not fit on the camera, nor will SQ-Ai cranks fit on the earlier models.

SQ-B. The SQ-B was introduced as a low-cost, completely manual version of the SQ-Ai. It takes all lenses and finders from the SQ series, but won't offer metering or automatic exposure with the AE prisms.

Bronica SQ Lenses. Older lenses are designated S, and current lenses are designated PS. As with the ETR lenses, the current PS lenses are all computer designed, and all S and PS lenses will work on any SQ-series body. Lenses include: 35mm f3.5 fisheye, 40mm f3.5, 50mm f3.5, 65mm f4, 80mm f2.8, 110mm f4, 110mm f4.5 Macro, 135mm f4, 150mm f4, 180mm f4.5, 200mm f4.5, 250mm f5.6, and 500mm f8 (both S and PS).

Bronica GS-1. The GS-1 was the first camera to be designed and built in Bronica's new factory in the

early 1980s. Aside from being the first 6x7 SLR camera reasonable enough to consider for field use and the first Bronica to offer TTL/OTF flashmetering, all PG lenses were computer designed and built using the latest manufacturing technology. The PS and PE

The GS-1 was the first camera to be designed and built in Bronica's new factory in the early 1980s. Photo courtesy of Bronica.

lenses for the SQ and ETR cameras followed shortly under the same strict quality control used with the PQ lenses. Film backs on the GS-1 are nonrotating, so the use of a prism finder is highly recommended. The AE Rotary Prism is particularly noteworthy. Aside from adding automatic exposure, the finder rotates to allow waist–level-type viewing in both horizontal and vertical formats, making the camera extremely easy to handle even without a grip. To increase ease of use, an ISO dial is incorporated into the film back, and will automatically set the meter in the AE prisms to the correct ISO without having to reset anything on the camera. Thus, you can switch from 100 to 400 speed film and the meter will automatically adjust. For anyone looking for a 6x7 camera to use in the field, the GS-1 is an excellent choice. The leaf-shutter lenses also makes the GS-1 an excellent studio camera.

Bronica GS-1 Lenses. All lenses are PG, and include: 50mm f4.5, 65mm f4, 80mm f3.5, 100mm f3.5, 110mm f4, 150mm f4, 200mm f4.5, 250mm f5.6, and 500mm f8.

Contax 645. When first introduced, the Contax 645 was met with a combination of anticipation and apprehension. With autofocus and advanced metering modes, the 645 looked to combine a number of features previously seen only in 35mm cameras with the interchangeable finders and backs common to medium format. On the other hand, the 645 is Contax's first foray into modern medium format SLRs, and thus does not have a long proven track record like the products of most companies manufacturing medium format cameras. However, with access to Zeiss lenses, a horde of modern features, and backing from one of the most well-known names in serious photography, the Contax 645 is definitely a camera to consider.

Part of what sets the Contax apart from other medium format systems is the advanced metering and autofocus. Unlike a number of current systems where you must mount a prism or special finder to get autoexposure, you have access to both autofocus and all metering modes even if you use the waist-level finder. The reason for this is that the electronics have been built into the camera, rather than into accessory finders. However, Contax also chose to allow the option of interchangeable finders, rather than simply using a fixed prism finder as seen in the Pentax 645n and the Mamiya 645AF. Certain film backs also use Contax's vacuum system for ultimate film flatness—a system proven very effective in the 35mm Contax RTS-III. Combine this with access to the best Zeiss lenses, and the Contax makes an excellent (though somewhat pricey) camera.

With autofocus and advanced metering modes, the 645 combines a number of features previously seen only in 35mm cameras with the interchangeable finders and backs common to medium format. Photo courtesy of Contax.

Contax 645 Lenses. The following lenses (all Carl Zeiss with T* coating) are available: 35mm f3.5 Distagon (fisheye), 45mm f2.8 Distagon, 80mm f2.0 Planar, 120mm f4 Apo-Makro-Planar140mm, f2.8 Sonnar, and 210mm f4 Sonnar.

Fuji GX680. Fuji's sole offering in the SLR field is the nonstandard GX680-III. Unlike most current SLR cameras, which are designed for field use, the GX680-III is designed as a studio camera, with movements to control perspective and bellows focusing. However, with AE prisms and SLR viewing, the GX680-III offers greater ease of use than a traditional view camera. Current models have been updated to accept a variety of film formats, with backs ranging from 645 up to 6x8.

In terms of compatibility with older models, all previous GX lenses may be used with current bodies, and older cameras can use the latest GX M series lenses. Previous film holders are compatible with all models, but will not provide barcode scanning or multi-format capabilities. New models use CR123A batteries, where 680 and 680II models use specific battery packs.

"Hasselblad's entry level cameras are rugged mechanical workhorses..."

In all, the GX680 cameras offer a unique option for the studio photographer looking for greater image control, but who does not want a full view camera or the expense of 4x5 negatives.

Fuji GX680 Bodies. *GX680-III.* Features multi-format capability, and backs offering barcode scanning to automatically set ISO, as well as motor drive advance, and full front movements (tilt, shift, rise, fall).

GX680-S. This model is the same as the GX680-III, but without front movements.

Fuji GX680 Lenses. Available lenses include: 50mm f5.6, 65mm f5.6, 80mm f5.6, 100mm f4, 115mm f3.2, 125mm f5.6, 125mm f3.2, 135mm f5.6, 150mm f4.5, 180mm f5.6, 180mm f3.2, 210mm f5.6, 300mm f6.3, 190mm f8 SF, and 100-200 f5.6 zoom.

Hasselblad. Just as Rolleiflex is synonymous with the best twin lens reflexes, Hasselblad has earned a reputation as the premier medium format

manufacturer. With rugged reliability and a full compliment of Zeiss lenses to match, Hasselblad has often been the camera of choice for professionals moving into medium format. The quality of Hasselblad equipment is unquestionable; they are considered the standard of comparison in medium format—and for good reason.

Hasselblad's entry-level cameras, the 500 and 501 series, are rugged mechanical workhorses that have a very long and well proven track record. Even many of the original 500C bodies produced in the late 1950s are still in active use today, and with full service and support widely available—a feat not even matched by the legendary Rolleiflex TLR cameras. Upper models in the 500 series offer TTL flashmetering and motorized advance, yet the Hasselblad line is not limited only to mechanical cameras. The 200 and 2000 series cameras, with focal-plane shutters offering speeds up to $1/2000$ second, offer the latest in built-in meters, autoexposure modes, and access to the F-series lenses.

With such reliability, and access to some of the best lenses in medium format, why have some people nicknamed Hasselblad cameras "*Hassle*blads"? This derives from the one weak point in the 500 series line—the tendency to jam occasionally. The jam is not a catastrophic failure of the camera, and almost always results from operator error (the photographer accidentally fires the shutter while removing the lens, or when a cocked lens is mounted on an uncocked body). In some cases, the body can be unjammed on the spot by a knowledgeable Hasselblad owner, but taking it in for professional service is recommended, as you can easily damage the camera if you aren't extremely careful. Given that it usually takes a repairman a few moments to solve the problem (less than ten minutes in most cases), the repair charge is minimal and you can rest assured the camera will not be damaged. But because of this occasional hassle, the nickname "Hassleblad" resulted. Provided you take care to make sure lens, body, and back are all cocked and properly set before mounting or changing lenses or backs, and you take care not to fire the shutter when changing lenses, you should not have any problems with the camera.

Aside from the occasional jams caused by user error, Hasselblad cameras remain among the most reliable cameras of any type. While commonly seen in repair shops for simple cleaning and lubrication necessary after heavy professional use, catastrophic failures requiring major repairs are not as common with Hasselblad cameras as other brands.

Perhaps the greatest weakness of the Hasselblad system is also its greatest strength. In general, Hasselblad equipment is among the most expensive to buy—both new or used. While you can find an old 500C with lens and film back for around $1000 used, additional lenses tend to be significant investments. On the other hand, this also works in your favor. Of all current medium format systems, Hasselblad equipment holds its value better than any other brand. Many stores and photographers are willing to pay a premium for used equipment in good condition. While Hasselblad equipment can be pricier than other brands, there is no question that your investment provides you with the very best medium format has to offer, even with older equipment.

Hasselblad 202FA. Photo courtesy of Hasselblad

Hasselblad Bodies. *500C.* A completely manual, completely mechanical workhorse, it eclipsed the Rolleiflex as the camera of choice for professionals following its introduction in 1957. The body remains compatible with the vast majority of current lenses and accessories. However, due to a different shutter-cocking system, the earliest models may not be compatible with current CF lenses without an internal upgrade. With long lenses (those over 150mm), there is some viewfinder blackout.

500C/M: This is the same basic camera as the 500C, but with interchangeable focusing screens added.

500 Classic. A specially packaged version of the 500C/M sold with 80mm CF and A12 back.

501C. An updated version of the 500C/M, the 501C also offered the new Accumatte screen as standard equipment. Sold only in a kit with special C lens and A12 back.

501C/M. This model adds Hasselblad's new Gliding Mirror System to prevent vignetting in the viewfinder when using telephoto lenses.

503CX. The 503CX adds TTL/OTF flashmetering, but operates like a 500C/M in all other respects.

503CXi. An upgrade of the 503CX, the 503CXi is compatible with the Winder CW for motorized advance, and offers TTL/OTF flashmetering.

503CW. Features TTL/OTF flashmetering, compatiblity with Winder CW, and Gliding Mirror System.

500EL. This is a motorized version of the 500C.

500EL/M. This motorized version of the 500C/M offers interchangeable focusing screens.

500ELX. This model adds TTL/OTF flashmetering, and a larger mirror to prevent vignetting with telephoto lenses.

553ELX. An upgrade of the 500ELX, the 553ELX offers TTL/OTF flashmetering and is powered by 5 AA batteries, unlike previous models that required power packs.

555ELD. This model includes an integrated databus connection for digital backs, front release port for digital backs, and is compatible with an optional infrared remote trigger.

2000FC. The 2000FC includes essentially the same features as the 500 C/M, except with an electronically controlled focal plane shutter with speeds to $1/2000$ second. Additionally, the mirror can be locked up, set to return on film advance (as with the 500 models), or return instantly after exposure. The camera will take either C/CF or F lenses.

2000FC/M. This model is the same as the 2000FC, except with the provision to automatically retract the shutter curtain when the film back is removed to prevent accidental damage.

2000FCW. The 2000FCW is the same as the 2000FC/M, but with a removable wind crank to allow the 2000FCW motor drive to be attached.

2003FCW. This features mainly cosmetic improvements over the 2000FCW.

205TCC. TTL/OTF flashmetering, 1° spotmeter in camera, provisions for the Zone System, multi-mode aperture priority, mirror lockup, and an electronically controlled shutter with speeds from $1/2000$ second to 34 minutes rounds out the impressive feature list of the camera. Compatible with all Hasselblad lenses and the Winder F.

205FCC. This is an electronic upgrade of the 205TCC.

203FE. This model features TTL exposure using a 20° partial spotmeter, and TTL/OTF flashmetering. It is compatible with CF and FE lenses (both with focal plane shutter or with leaf shutter in CF lenses). The top shutter speed is $1/2000$ second. Mirror lockup, compatibility with the Winder F, and state of the art automatic exposure control round out the camera.

201F: Features TTL/OTF flashmetering and a top shutter speed of $1/1000$ second, but no meter.

202FA. This scaled-back version of the 203FE will take FE, CFE, or CF/CFi/CFE lenses (CF lenses in focal plane shutter mode only), but will not take C or CB lenses. The model features shutter speeds from 34 minutes to $1/1000$ second, with TTL/OTF flashmetering. Standard metering is TTL using a 20° partial metering area. Includes automatic exposure capability built-in, mirror lockup, and takes the Winder F.

Hasselblad Lenses. *C (original)/CF(later)/CFi (i=improved CF)/CB(like Cfi, but cannot be used with 202FA or Arcbody)/CFE(latest with electronic data transfer)(Carl Zeiss T* unless otherwise noted).* 30mm f3.5 fisheye, 40mm f4, 50mm f4, 60mm f3.5, 80mm f2.8, 100mm f3.5, 120mm f4 Makro, 135mm f5.6, 150mm f4, 160mm f4.8, 180mm f4, 250mm f5.6, 350mm f5.6, 500mm f8, and 140–280mm f5.6 Schneider Variogon.

F/FE (with electronic data transfer) (Carl Zeiss T* unless otherwise noted). 50mm f2.8, 80mm f2.8, 110 f2.0, Hasselblad 60–120 f4.8, 150mm f2.8, 250mm f4, 350mm f4.

Teleconverters. 1.4x, 1.4x APO, 2x, 1.4x PC Mutar with shift (works with 40mm-100mm lenses).

Hasselblad Wide Angle Bodies. *Supreme Wide Angle, SWA/SW.* This camera features a 38mm f4.5 Zeiss Biogon lens that must be cocked before each exposure.

☐ A Note on Classic Hasselblads

In looking at medium format camera listings, you may come across the listings for the original Hasselblad SLRs, the 1000F and 1600F. While the Ektar lenses available for the cameras are quite good, the cameras are not compatible with current Hasselblad systems, nor are these cameras as reliable as the current cameras. Shutter problems are not uncommon with the camera, and both Hasselblad and photographers consider these early cameras collector's items, since parts and repairs are difficult to obtain. However, if you find one in good working order, it is an option to consider when looking for a medium format SLR on a budget.

The cameras are focal plane shutter models. The distinguishing feature between the 1000F and 1600F is the top shutter speed—the 1600 tops out at $1/1600$ second, while the 1000 tops out at $1/1000$ second. Contrary to logical progression, the 1000 was actually the later model. It should also be noted that the current Kiev 88 SLR is actually a copy of these early Hasselblads. To the credit of the Russians, many of the Russian lenses are top notch. The shutter on the Kiev 88 is far more reliable than that of the classic Hasselblads, but overall quality on the Russian cameras varies highly—some are workhorses that never break, while others have light leaks, rough finishes, and mechanical problems galore. In all, the classic Hasselblad cameras (and their modern Russian kin) are options to consider only if on a budget—and if you can accept the greater possibility the camera will require repairs.

SWC. An upgrade of the Supreme Wide Angle, the SWC automatically cocks the shutter when the film is advanced.

SWC/M (1980-1982). This and all later models are compatible with the Polaroid magazines.

SWC/M (1982-1986). This model receives a CF lens upgrade, and old-style viewfinder.

SWC/M (1986-1988). A CF lens and new-style viewfinder are featured.

903SWC. Largely cosmetic changes are made.

Mamiya. Like their TLR and rangefinder offerings, the Mamiya SLR cameras offer solid quality and good value. The RB and RZ cameras, in particular, have earned stellar reputations as studio cameras, with sharp lenses and excellent reliability. Those on a budget should seriously consider older models as a way to both enter a Mamiya system and an opportunity to obtain top-quality results at a reasonable cost. Because older cameras can use current lenses, They work exceptionally well as backup cameras. For both professional and amateur photography, the Mamiya SLR cameras make excellent choices.

Perhaps the most popular choice in the 645 format, Mamiya has remained a leader in 645 since introducing the world's first 645 SLR in the mid-1970s. While not quite as modular as the Bronica ETR system, Mamiya offers an extensive array of film backs and accessories, and also offers the most extensive line of lenses in medium format. The 300mm f2.8 and 500mm f4.5 are the only ones currently available in medium format, giving Mamiya an edge in nature photography and other applications where fast, long telephotos are advantageous. All cameras feature focal plane shutters, giving them a definite lean towards field work. However, a number of leaf shutter lenses are available should you need them for outdoor fill flash or studio applications.

The older 645 cameras are particularly noteworthy. While they will not take current finders, and use film inserts instead of film backs, the older 645 models offer exceptional reliability and make excellent choices for the professional or amateur on a budget.

Mamiya 645 Bodies. *645.* A very robust camera, some have commented that they think the early Mamiya 645 models (the 645, 645J, and 645 1000s) are better built than the current cameras. The 645 offers mirror lockup, instant return mirror (no blackout after taking a shot), compatibility with metered and AE prisms, as well as various grips and a motor drive. Shutter speeds range from eight seconds to $^1/_{500}$ second (all quartz controlled).

645J. A stripped-down version of the original 645, it was intended as a low-cost alternative to the full 645. Features such as mirror lockup and compatibility with the AE prism were removed, as were the two-, four-, and eight-second shutter speeds. Like the original 645, the top shutter speed is $^1/_{500}$ second. An incredibly basic but very reliable model, the 645J is a solid value for entry into the Mamiya 645 system due to its relatively low price.

645 1000s. This model has essentially the same features as the original 645, but with a top shutter speed of $^1/_{1000}$ second. It is compatible with all early viewfinders, but to use the $^1/_{1000}$ second speed with a metered prism, you need to have the PDs version. When using the older PD metered prism, the top shutter speed available is $^1/_{500}$ second (unless you set the camera manually). This model also offers a self timer.

645 Super. A complete redesign of the 645, the Super brings a number of new features, such as compatibility with the new AE prisms with different metering modes. The camera was updated to take film backs instead of simply film inserts, greatly increasing their ease of use and offering the option to change film types in mid-roll. Focusing screens are also interchangeable.

> ## "The RB and RZ cameras have earned stellar reputations as studio cameras..."

645 Pro. An upgrade of the Super, the film transport was improved to eliminate problems caused in the Super by thick emulsion films such as T-Max. An electronic interface for the new leaf shutter lenses and a self timer were also added.

645 Pro TL. TTL flashmetering is added to the 645 Pro.

645 AF. The newest camera in the series, the 645 AF introduces autofocus and more advanced metering modes. However, the 645 AF does not offer interchangeable finders like previous models. Instead, you have a fixed prism finder.

645E. This is a stripped-down version of the 645 Pro. It takes film inserts only (like the early 645 models), and offers an integrated but non-interchangeable AE prism finder. Mamiya offers a winder for this model that is virtually the same as the Speed Grip produced by Bronica for their current SLR cameras. Currently the lowest cost medium format SLR you can purchase new, but in my opinion, the overall limitations in design and lower construction quality (compared to the 645 Pro TL or 645 AF) make it best attuned to amateur use, or as a backup to a full Mamiya 645 system. A good option for a new camera if you are on a budget and insist on new equipment, but the original 645 or 645 1000s may be a better option due to better construction quality and a wider range of accessories and finders.

Mamiya 645 Lenses. The following lenses are available: 24mm f4 fisheye, 35mm f3.5, 45mm f2.8, 50mm f4 Shift, 55mm f2.8, 55mm f2.8 LS, 70mm f2.8 LS, 80mm f1.9, 80mm f2.8, 80mm f2.8 LS, 80mm f4 Macro, 120mm f4 Macro, 150mm f2.8, 150mm f3.8 LS, 200mm f2.8 APO, 300mm f5.6, 300mm f2.8 APO, 500mm f5.6, 500mm f4.5 APO, 55-110mm f4.5, and 105-210mm f4.5.

Mamiya 645 AF Lenses. The following lenses are available: 45mm f2.8, 55mm f2.8, 80mm f2.8, 150mm f2.8, 210mm f4, and 300mm f4.5.

"The leaf shutter in all the lenses makes them ideal for studio work."

Mamiya RB and RZ67. Considered by many the studio camera of choice, the RB and RZ cameras offer a wide range of lenses and accessories. With bellows focusing, the cameras can also be used for close-up work. The leaf shutter in all the lenses makes them ideal for studio work. Lenses are all top notch and, combined with the 6x7 negatives, can provide images that surpass those from 645 and 6x6 cameras. The rotating film back provides a unique solution to the question of horizontal and vertical shooting. Rather than rotate the camera, you rotate the film back, making life much easier—particularly if you are working on a tripod. On the other hand, field work is not particularly easy due to the size and weight of the cameras. In all, the RB and RZ are among the best in medium format today, and offer negatives in the size many current art directors prefer.

The main difference between the RB and RZ cameras is in electronics. The RB series cameras are completely mechanical cameras, with no electronics or autoexposure capabilities. The RZ, on the other hand, includes a full set of electronics, giving the photographer access to features such as autoexposure and automatic ISO setting by the film back. Both cameras are exceptional workhorses, and offer the photographer the option of both electronically controlled exposure with the RZ or completely mechanical control with the RB.

Mamiya RB67 Bodies. *RB67.* This is an all-mechanical workhorse with *no* electronic parts or accessories (except for the PD metered prism). It features interchangeable focusing screens, bellows focusing, and film backs from 645 to 6x8, and Polaroid. Shutter cocking and film advance are separate.

RB67 Pro-S. This model adds double exposure prevention, a one-touch focusing hood, and an automatic frame-line indicator when the back is in the horizontal position.

RB67 Pro-SD. The Pro-S body is improved to accept 75mm shift and 500mm APO lenses.

Mamiya RB67 Lenses. *The following lenses are available:* 37mm f4.5, 50mm f4.5, 65mm f4.0, 75mm f3.5, 75mm f4.5 shift, 90mm f3.5, 127mm f3.5, 140mm f4.5 Macro, 150mm f3.5, 150mm f4 SF, 180mm f4.5, 210mm f4.5, 250mm f4.5, 250mm f4.5 APO, 350mm f5.6 APO, 500mm f8, 500mm f6 APO, and 100–200mm f5.2.

Mamiya RZ67 Bodies. *RZ67.* This is an electronically upgraded RB67 with electronic shutter, single stroke shutter cocking and film advance, interlocking AE prism, and compatibility with all RB and RZ lenses.

RZ67-II: This model is an upgrade of the original RZ67. Step shutter speeds, micro-fine focusing, and internal diagnostic circuitry were added.

Mamiya RZ67 Lenses. The following lenses are available: 37mm f4.5, 50mm f4.5, 65mm f4.0, 75mm f4.5 shift, 90mm f3.5, 110mm f2.8, 140mm f4.5 Macro, 150mm f3.5, 180mm f4.5, 210mm f.45 APO, 250mm f4.5, 250mm f4.5 APO, 350mm f5.6 APO, 500mm f8, 500mm f6 APO, and 100–200mm f5.2.

Pentax. Since the advent of the universal screw mount and the Spotmatic cameras, Pentax has remained one of the leading strongest photographic manufacturers. Like the Pentax 35mm cameras, their medium format cameras have always been of excellent quality at very competitive prices. The 6x7 camera system, in particular, has a well-deserved reputation for good quality at prices below equivalent equipment from other manufacturers. Pentax has also been a leader in medium format, introducing the world's first autofocus medium format SLR system with the 645n.

In looking at Pentax's current 645 and 6x7 systems, there are a number of obvious differences. The Pentax 645 cameras offer built-in motor drives, autoexposure modes, film inserts for fast loading, and a horde of features you would expect to find only in a 35mm camera. This, combined with the relatively low cost of additional lenses, has made the Pentax 645 system a favorite for those stepping into medium format from advanced 35mm systems.

The 6x7 cameras, on the other hand, resemble overgrown 35mm cameras, both in features and operation. Rather than using a film insert system, the 6x7 cameras use a horizontal film transport with single-action advance (via lever), like those found on a manual focus 35mm camera. The 6x7 system has also been dominated by all-mechanical bodies, which have become favorites of professionals and amateurs seeking a completely manual 6x7 camera. With the 6x7-II, Pentax now brings autoexposure to the system, increasing the versatility of the system.

Unlike other medium format manufacturers, Pentax has also made available a number of long telephoto lenses for use with their cameras. For the 645 system, there is a 600mm f5.6. The 6x7 system has a whopping 800mm f4 available—one of the fastest long telephoto lenses in medium format. While these lenses are neither small nor cheap, they are in many cases similar in price and size to long telephotos for 35mm cameras—a feat not matched by any other manufacturer. Mamiya offers a number of fast telephotos, but at prices well over $10,000. Most of the Pentax telephotos can be had for significantly less.

Overall, both systems have much to offer both amateurs and professionals, yet there are a few drawbacks to keep in mind. With the 645 system, the prism finder is not interchangeable and the camera takes film inserts rather than film backs. Thus, if you prefer to occasionally use a waist-level finder or need to change film types mid-roll, it cannot be done with the Pentax 645 cameras. With the 6x7, the bulk and weight of the camera make it a bear to use hand held. Additionally, the mirror slap on these cameras is significant, and mirror lockup is recommended at all times, if possible. I once heard a Pentax 6x7 owner describe $1/8$ second and $1/15$ second as "the shutter speeds of death." At these speeds, the shutter causes noticeable vibration—even if the mirror is locked up. Like the 645s, the Pentax 6x7 cameras do not have interchangeable film backs, so mid-roll film changes without wasting film is not possible. The final drawback of the Pentax cameras is in the use of Polaroid

Pentax 645N with SMCP-FA 645 75mm f2.8 lens. Photo courtesy of Pentax.

backs. Should you be interested in using Polaroid film to shoot proofs, you must buy and dedicate a Pentax body to using only Polaroid film. Additionally, this conversion is not cheap and available only from NPC, a third-party manufacturer of Polaroid backs. However, if like most photographers you don't use Polaroid backs, don't need to change film mid-roll, and don't plan on using a wide variety of finders, the Pentax systems are excellent options, and at very reasonable prices to boot.

Pentax 645 Bodies. *645.* This electronic body offers multiple auto and manual exposure modes, including aperture-priority, shutter priority, and program modes. The prism finder is non-interchangeable. The camera features interchangeable film inserts, and a built-in motor drive advance. It includes interchangeable focusing screens, and film inserts in 120, 220, and 70mm bulk load. Semiautomatic film load and auto rewind are featured, with TTL flash and programmed auto flash modes.

645n. This model is similar to the original 645, but adds autofocus and multiple metering modes.

Pentax 645 Lenses. All current. FA lenses are autofocus capable. It should also be noted that

Pentax 67-II body with 105mm f2.4 lens. Photo courtesy of Pentax.

Pentax 6x7 lenses may also be used on the 645 cameras by using an adaptor readily available from Pentax.

SMC Pentax-A (non-AF). Lenses include: 35mm f3.5, 45mm f2.8, 55mm f2.8, 75mm f2.8, 120mm f4 Macro, 150mm f3.5, 200mm f4, 300mm f4, 600mm f5.6, 45–85mm f4.5, 80–160mm f4.5, 75mm f2.5 leaf shutter, 135mm f4 leaf shutter, 1.4x teleconverter, and 2x teleconverter.

SMC Pentax-FA (AF). Lenses include: 45mm f2.8, 75mm f2.8, 300mm f4, and 400mm f5.6. More are planned, but were not yet available at the time of writing.

Pentax 6x7 Bodies. *6x7.* This is a completely mechanical body. With the TTL metered prism, it is literally the Pentax K-1000 of medium format in terms of features and operation. Note that the TTL prism must be mounted with the lens off the body for proper meter coupling (true of all later models as well). Due to lack of mirror lockup, this is the least desirable body.

6x7 MLU. Mirror lockup is added, which is highly recommended.

67. This model is basically the same in features and operation as the 6x7 MLU.

67-II. This complete update to the Pentax 6x7 series offers access to an AE prism for aperture-priority automatic exposure. It will not take the earlier TTL prism, but will accept all other accessories and finders. Likewise, the AE prism cannot be used on earlier models.

Pentax 6x7 Lenses. *Super Takumar (oldest), SMC (Super Multicoated) Takumar (later), SMC Pentax (current).* These lenses include: 45mm f4, 55mm f4, 75mm f4.5, 75mm f4.5 Shift, 90mm f2.8, 100mm f4 Macro, 105mm f2.4, 120mm f3.5 Soft Focus, 135mm f4 Macro, 165mm f2.8, 165mm f4 Leaf-Shutter, 200mm f4, 300mm f4, 400mm f4, 500mm f5.6, 600mm f4, 800mm f4, 800mm f6.7, 1000mm f8 Mirror, and 55–100mm f4.5

Rollei. With Rollei's long history in the photographic world, it is not surprising that the current SLR cameras offered by them rank among the very best available in medium format. The current SLR offerings from Rollei are, however, somewhat different from the mechanical TLR workhorses that forged their reputation. The 6000 series cameras are among the most sophisticated cameras in photography today, with truly extensive feature lists. The 6008 Integral has not only a built-in motor drive that moves at 2.5 fps (one of the fastest in medium format today) and a large number of autoexposure modes, but also features the ability to take and average multiple spotmeter readings in the camera. With innovative and advanced cameras, Rollei remains on the cutting edge of medium format.

In addition to its bodies, Rollei also offers an extensive list of accessories for the 6000 series cameras. The Rollei film backs are reputed to offer the best film flatness of all current medium format systems, matched only by the special vacuum seal back available for the Contax 645. Standard film backs include 6x6, a rotating 645 back, and Polaroid—but the true star of the Rollei film backs is the impressive array of digital backs available for the system.

Lenses range from 30mm up to 1000mm, and include a number of zooms, teleconverters, and special purpose lenses. Rollei further extends the usefulness of the system with two bellows/view cameras that take 6000 series lenses and accessories—the X-Act2 and the 6000 PCS.

In all, the Rollei 6000 system is one of the most complete in medium format, and offers a great deal to the professional and serious amateur photographer for both field and studio use.

For those seeking a mechanical system, Rollei also offers the SL66 series cameras. These bodies offer focal plane shutters, bellows focusing with 50mm extension (for close-up work), tilt for depth of field control, and a number of lenses that can be reverse-mounted on the body for extreme close-up work. The SL66 series cameras are unique in medium format, and offer a great deal. As icing on the cake, the system uses Zeiss lenses from 30mm up to 1000mm and a good range of film backs, including 6x6, 645, and Polaroid. As a result of the tilt and bellows focusing, the SL 66 cameras are particularly well suited for studio and technical work.

The only major downsides to the current Rollei systems are price and availability. Prices for new bodies are among the most expensive in medium format,

exceeded only by the Hasselblad 200 series cameras. Lenses are also on the expensive side, with the Rollei/Zeiss lenses tending to be roughly the same cost as their Hasselblad counterparts (which are decidedly not cheap). Rollei also offers a number of high speed and special purpose lenses made by Schneider; among them are the 80mm f2 Xenotar, 180mm f2.8 Tele-Xenar, two zooms, and the 55mm PC Super Angulon with tilt/shift capabilities, but these lenses also tend to come at heftier prices than the Zeiss glass.

Perhaps the largest problem is that of availability. Rollei SLR equipment can be a bit difficult to find—either new, used, or for rent (particularly with the SL66 series). If you take a look through the advertisements in *Shutterbug* magazine, you will find a great number of listings for the TLR cameras, but relatively few for the 6000 series SLRs—and possibly no listings at all for the SL66 cameras. However, if you are looking for the very best medium format has to offer, it is definitely worth the search for any of the fine Rollei SLRs.

"Rollei SLR equipment can be a bit difficult to find—either new, used, or for rent."

Rollei SLX/6000 Series Bodies. All bodies use specific rechargeable Nicad batteries, and care should be taken to ensure that the correct battery is used. An SLX battery, for example, can damage a 6000 series camera. A number of major and minor differences exist between bodies (and variations of models), and listing them all is impossible. Sources also tend to conflict a bit—one source on the 6006 cameras mentions only a difference in multiple exposure capability between the Mk. I and Mk. II versions, while another source lists a difference in the shutter button design, fuse used by the camera, and an improved screen on the Mk. II. For all the exact differences between models, I recommend contacting Rollei directly.

SLX (Mark 1). This is the world's first microprocessor-controlled medium format SLR, introduced in 1973. It accepts most later lenses and accessories, except for PQS lenses with $1/1000$ second speed. Mirror lockup is achieved by use of special electronic shutter release. The mirror can cause problems—

when fired, the mirror creates a vacuum inside the body that can potentially shatter the mirror. This is not a constant problem with the camera, but happened frequently enough that Rollei quickly replaced the SLX with a Mark 2 version featuring a redesigned mirror. It will accept 6000 series inserts, but SLX inserts cannot be used on 6000 series cameras. 6008 backs should not be used on the SLX or damage could occur. SLX backs offer both 120 and 220 capability. Film cannot be changed mid-roll.

SLX (Mark 2). Provision for standard cable release on front of camera between the two shutter releases. Mirror problem fixed. Otherwise, the same as the SLX.

6001. This is a budget alternative to the 6003 Professional

The Rolleiflex 6008 (left) and 6001 (right). Photo courtesy of Rollei.

and 6008 Integral. The film advance is cut to 1.5 fps, and there is no built-in meter. TTL flashmetering is available using the Metz SCA-300 system. The body has mirror lockup and multiple exposure ability.

6001 HG. The same as the 6001, but this model also accepts the hand grip (hence the HG designation).

6002. Intended as a budget alternative to the 6006, it takes film backs but they cannot be changed mid-roll. Similar to the 6006, but without interchangeable backs. Introduced in 1985 with three low-cost Rolleigon lenses—50mm, 80mm, and 150mm. Will not take the 6008 backs.

6003 SRC 1000. Includes both center-weighted and spotmetering modes, open aperture metering with PQ and PQS lenses (previous models use stop-down metering), and adds aperture priority and programmed autoexposure modes (previous models only offered shutter priority for autoexposure). Autobracketing is also added (PQ and PQS lenses only), along with on-camera ISO setting. The body is gray.

6003 Professional. This model accepts the new hand grip, and offers an added on-camera mirror lockup button. Film ISO setting is done on the film

back, like the 6008. There is increased viewfinder information. The body color is changed to black, to match the 6008 Integral. There is a 2 fps motor drive advance. SLX and 6002 backs should not be used on the camera.

6006 (Mark 1). Includes center-weighted metering, built-in motor drive, shutter priority autoexposure, and interchangeable film backs. This model takes 6008 backs, but ISO is set on the camera, not the film back. To avoid fogging, do not change 6008 backs mid-roll on the 6006.

6006 (Mark 2). This model is the same as the 6006, but with provision for multiple exposures on the camera. It includes a brighter focusing screen.

6008. This is a major update of the 6006 design. It includes all features of the 6003 SRC 1000, plus film backs featuring ISO setting, which is transferred to the camera meter. Using older film backs from the 6006 causes the meter to default to ISO 100, but the wide range of exposure compensation allows the setting of other film speeds. Multispot metering is available. SLX and 6002 backs should not be used.

6008 SRC (Scan Remote Control) 1000. This is an upgrade of the 6008, now compatible with Rollei's Digital Scanpak back.

6008 Integral. This model features a 2.5fps motor drive—the fastest in medium format. Autobracketing is available in manual metering modes (autobracketing on all 6008 cameras requires PQ or PQS lenses). New system-checking circuitry. The largest enhancement is the ability to use the Master Control Unit for an amazing amount of control over the camera. The camera comes standard with Rollei's hand grip that makes handling the camera very easy.

Rollei SLX/6000 Lenses. All current lenses are designed by Schneider or Zeiss, and are top notch. A number of the Zeiss designs for Rollei are the same as those currently used by Hasselblad, but the Rollei lenses use Rollei's own HFT coating instead of the Zeiss T* coating. PQ and PQS are the current series, with the PQ being introduced in 1989 alongside the original 6008. PQS lenses offer a top shutter speed of $1/1000$ second, and are compatible only with the 6008 and later cameras with a marking for $1/1000$ second on the shutter dial (*Note:* not all 6008 cameras are PQS compatible). Earlier models without a setting for $1/1000$ second (SLX, 6002, 6006, etc.) should not be used with PQS lenses.

Zeiss. Lenses include: 30mm f3.5 Distagon, 40mm f4 Distagon, 60mm f3.5 Distagon, 80mm f2.8 Planar, 120mm f4 Makro-Planar, 150mm f4 Sonnar, 250mm f5.6 Sonnar, 350mm f5.6 Tele-Tessar, 500mm f8 Tele-Tessar, and 1000mm f8 Tele-Tessar.

Schneider. Lenses include: 40mm f3.5 Super-Angulon, 50mm f2.8 Super Angulon, 55mm f4.5 PC Super-Angulon, 80mm f2 Xenotar, 60mm f3.5 (discontinued), 80mm f2.8 Xenotar (discontinued), 90mm f4 APO-Symmar, 150mm f4 Tele-Xenar (discontinued), 180mm f2.8 Tele-Xenar, 300mm f4 APO Tele-Xenar, 75-150mm f4.5 Variogon, and 140-280mm f5.6 Variogon.

Rolleigon. These lenses, made for Rollei by Mamiya, are no longer in production. They include: 50mm f4, 80mm f2.8, and 150mm f4.

Rollei SL 66 Series Bodies. *SL 66.* A tilting front is standard. Features a completely modular design, and relatively quiet operation on an all-mechanical body with very solid construction.

SL 66E. This model adds built-in exposure metering and TTL flashmetering to the SL 66.

SL 66X. This economy version of the SL 66E lacks a built-in exposure meter but still retains TTL flashmetering.

SL66SE. An upgrade of the SL 66E, it adds built-in spotmetering. DOF scales on the body can be set for the 50mm, 80mm, 150mm, and 250mm lenses.

Rollei SL 66 Series Lenses. These lenses (all Zeiss) include: 30mm f3.5 F-Distagon (Fisheye), 40mm f4 Distagon, 50mm f4 Distagon, 60mm f3.5 Distagon, 80mm f2.8 Planar, 80mm f4 Distagon Leaf-Shutter, 120mm f4 Makro-Planar, 150mm f4 Sonnar, 250mm f5.6 Sonnar, 500mm f5.6 Tele-Tessar, 1000mm f8 Tele-Tessar, 1000mm f5.6 Mirotar (mirror lens, fully corrected for infrared use), and 2x teleconverter.

> **"All current lenses are designed by Schneider or Zeiss, and are top-notch."**

An adaptor ring for using view camera lenses is also available, as is a shift adaptor for view camera lenses, and an adaptor to accept Schneider M-Componon Magnifying Lenses. 50mm, 60mm, 80mm, and 120mm Makro-Planar lenses can all be reverse-mounted on the body for extreme close-up work—up to a 3:1 ratio with the 50mm lens.

Chapter 6

Other Medium Format Cameras

As if the wide selection of SLRs, TLRs, and rangefinders wasn't enough, medium format also offers a wide range of specific cameras for technical and special use. View cameras, field cameras, technical cameras, and true panoramic cameras are all readily available. Even for photographers with very specialized needs, chances are there is a medium format camera that will cover the task perfectly.

☐ Field and View Cameras

For architectural photography, macro photography, or any other situation where perspective control is required, a field or view camera is the ideal choice.

Perspective control lenses are available for most medium format SLR systems, yet they tend to be expensive, rather sizeable beasts, and offer only limited perspective control. Medium format field and view cameras will provide much more extensive movements and also offer a more cost-effective alternative to a 4x5 camera. Lenses and cameras are similar in cost to large format, but film and developing costs (which constitute 90% of a photographer's expenses) are greatly reduced by using roll film. Additionally, since medium format images require smaller lens coverage, you can use lenses such as the 35mm Rodenstock Grandagon, which provides an image on 6x9 format that is roughly equivilent to an 18mm ultrawide on a 35mm camera. Since the image circle of the 35mm Grandagon is 125mm while a 6x9 negative only requires a 104mm image circle, you still have room for limited movements.

The primary difference between field and view cameras is the range of movements offered on the camera. View cameras offer complete movements (rise, fall, tilt, shift), and also the most extreme movements, for complete image control. Field cameras still offer movements, but they may be extremely limited as seen on baby Speed Graphics. With field cameras like the Linhof Super Techina 23, the difference between field and view cameras narrows considerably, though. The Linhof provides extensive movements that will cover the vast majority of situations.

The other advantage to view cameras is their ability to use digital backs. Linhof's M679 6x9/digital view camera is designed and built for use with the best digital backs. These require extremely rigid cameras as they scan the subject three times—once for each color (RGB).

If you're looking for complete perspective control or the ability to use the best digital backs in the studio, a field or view camera would be best.

☐ Field and View Camera Terminology

Tilt: The ability to tilt either the lens or film forwards or backwards. Used primarily for depth of field control.

Shift: The ability to move the lens or film plane laterally. This provides perspective control to correct horizontal lines so that they appear parallel on film. On "tilt/shift" perspective control lenses for SLR cameras, the shift refers to the ability to shift the lens either horizontally or vertically.

Rise and Fall: The ability to raise or lower the lens or film plane vertically. Used to make vertical lines appear parallel on film and perspective control.

Standard: Refers to the front or back of the camera. The front standard is where the lens attaches and the rear standard is where the film back or ground glass is attached.

☐ Field and View Camera Models

Hasselblad Arcbody and Flexbody. Developed by Hasselblad for those who need movements in the studio or for architectural work, the Arc- and Flexbodies offer a solid alternative to investing in a field or view camera. Each offers tilt and shift for depth of field control in packages significantly more compact than a standard view camera. Additionally, both cameras take Hasselblad film backs and viewfinders, and the Flexbody also takes standard Hasselblad lenses, increasing its usefulness to those who have already invested in a Hasselblad system. However, due to the relatively small image circles of standard Hasselblad lenses, perspective control is limited. The Arcbody, billed as a technical camera, uses Rodenstock Grandagon lenses, which allow for greater movements and image control. In either case, the Arc- and Flexbodies offer tremendous capability in compact packages, with the added bonus of compatibility with current Hasselblad acessories.

Rollei X-Act2. Looking for a full view camera, but want one that is compact and is in 6x6 format? Then the Rollei X-Act2 is exactly what you want. This extremely sophisticated view camera offers full movements and can take the Rollei digital film back for high quality digital studio work. The camera will take either Rollei PQ lenses or specially mounted large format lenses. With the control unit, you obtain an amazing degree of control over exposure and camera functionality, making it a very sophisticated view camera. Rollei also offers an impressive array of digital backs for the camera for serious studio use. For serious technical photography in 6x6 format, the Rollei is definitely one to be considered.

Rollei X-Act2. Photo courtesy of Rollei.

Linhof Super Technika 23 and M679. These cameras represent the pinnacle of 6x9 field and view cameras. The Technika comes from the long line of Technika and Master Technika 4x5 cameras that helped make Linhof famous, and the Super Technika 23 continues this fine tradition. A relatively light and compact field camera, lenses can also be adjusted to work with the Technika's coupled rangefinder for focusing. With the generous movements provided, the Technika makes for a great location camera for architecture and landscapes. If you require a portable camera with extensive perspective control, the Super Technika 23 or something similar will work exceptionally well.

The M679, on the other hand, provides an excellent example of the best in studio cameras. It provides far more extensive movements than a field camera, with tilt, shift, and rise available on both the front and rear standards. The camera is also designed and built to the most rigid tolerances to accept digital film backs, making it an extremely valuable studio tool.

Linhof M679. Photo courtesy of Linhof.

□ Panoramic Cameras

Panoramic images have gained immense popularity of late, and it's easy to understand why. Particularly well suited to landscapes and travel photography, the images provide an extremely wide angle of view and often provide a unique and stunning perspective.

Panoramic cameras tend to be a little misunderstood, both in terms of perspective and actual film format. In looking at lenses, it can be difficult to figure out exactly what sort of coverage and effective view you will achieve. The 45mm lens on the Hasselblad X-pan, for example, provides a horizontal angle of view similar to that of a 24mm lens on a 35mm camera, but has a vertical angle of view that corresponds to that of a 45mm lens. While this makes life a little tricky when considering a panoramic camera, the most important spec to look at is the horizontal angle of view.

Film Format. Film format also causes confusion, particularly in terms of what constitutes "medium format." Since 6x12 and 6x17 cameras take 120 film, there is a tendency to consider them medium format. However, this is not the case. The 6x12 format requires a 4x5 enlarger to make prints, and 6x17 requires a 5x7 enlarger. If you plan to print your own negatives, keep this in mind. This is particularly true if you want to work with 6x17, since 5x7 enlargers are neither cheap nor easy to find. In general, any panoramic format that has negatives 70mm or shorter can be used without difficulty in a medium format enlarger.

Also take into careful consideration the film format and find the aspect ratio that you prefer. 6x12, for example, provides a 1:2 aspect ratio where 6x17 provides a longer 1:2.85 aspect ratio. In general, a 1:2 or similar aspect is a bit easier to work with, but does not provide as dramatic an effect as cameras with a 1:2.6 or longer aspect.

In looking at panoramic cameras, you will find two types. First are standard cameras, which use regular lenses. These cameras operate similarly to other cameras of the same type, but have a panoramic format instead. For the most part, current

(Top) Canadian Geese Marching, Federal Heights, CO.
(Bottom) Hancock Shaker Village, Pittsfield, MA.

panoramic cameras are predominantly viewfinder cameras, with a few rangefinders also available. The other major design of panoramic cameras is the rotating lens camera. By using a lens that rotates during exposure and employing a curved film plane, rotating lens panoramic cameras cover exceptionally wide angles of view and produce some of the most stunning panoramics. The rotating lens design has also been used in the Spinshot 35S camera, which takes complete 360 degree panoramic images.

☐ Panoramic Camera Models

Fuji GX617. Fuji's offering in panoramic cameras is the impressive GX617. With interchangeable lenses from 90mm to 300mm, the Fuji offers excellent quality and versatility, and is well respected by panoramic photographers. Current lenses for the camera are a 90mm f5.6, 105mm f8, 180mm f6.7, and 300mm f8, covering a range from superwide to short telephoto. A center filter is recommended for the 90mm and 105mm lenses to ensure even coverage on the negative. Focusing is done by scale on the lens, though you can get a ground glass for precise focus and framing.

Hasselblad X-Pan. A 35mm dual-format panoramic (24mm x 65mm) and standard (24mm x 36mm) camera, the X-Pan offers a great deal to photographers. The camera itself has a split-image rangefinder, with autoexposure interchangeable lenses—currently a 45mm and 90mm. An excellent and very compact panoramic camera, the success of the camera exceeded Hasselblad's expectations, and there were some problems with backordering when the camera was first introduced. For those looking for a relatively compact panoramic camera, the X-pan certainly provides an excellent option.

Horseman SW 612. With six lenses from 35mm through 90mm, the Horseman SW 612 offers the most lenses of any interchangeable lens panoramic camera. If you wish, you can also use 6x7 and 6x9 film holders rather than only 6x12, giving it added versatility. With the wide selection of lenses and film backs, the SW 612 is perhaps the most versatile of the current panoramic cameras, lacking only a mild telephoto lens.

Linhof. Linhof currently offers two panoramic cameras: the 612 PC-II and 617 S-III. Both are exceptionally well-built cameras with interchangeable lenses. The 612 PC-II features built-in rise for perspective control. With their Schneider lenses, the Linhof cameras are capable of truly exceptional images and severe damage to your bank account. However, if you can afford either of these fine cameras, you will be rewarded with some of the best images possible. Like the Fuji and Horseman, the Linhofs are viewfinder cameras with focusing done by scale on the lens.

Noblex. Noblex has made an art of the swing lens panoramic, offering tremendously wide angles of view on a variety of panoramic formats. Noblex currently offers three series of cameras: the 135, 150, and 175. The 135 takes 35mm film and offers a 136° angle of view on 24mm x 66mm negatives. The 150 offers a whopping 146° angle of view in a 2x4.5 format on 120 film. The 175 offers a 138° angle of view in 6x17 format. To give you an idea of scale, on a

Linhof Technorama 612 PCII. Photo courtesy of Linhof.

35mm camera, a 50mm lens has a 46° angle of view, a 14mm lens has a angle of view of 114°, and a fisheye lens has a 180° angle of view (but with severe distortion). The swing lens design of the Noblex cameras gives you an exceptionally wide angle of view (wider than that of a 14mm lens), but without the distortion. This makes the Noblex cameras ideal for stunning wide panoramic photographs.

Linhof Aerotronica 69. Photo courtesy of Linhof.

□ Conclusion

As if the availability of true panoramic cameras and field/view cameras weren't enough, a number of other medium format cameras are also available for extremely specialized needs. Hasselblad, for example, offers the MK-70 for photogrammetric survey and other technical applications, and Rollei also offers equipment for photogrammetric use. Linhof, Hasselblad, Mamiya, and others also offer aerial cameras or underwater housings (some made by third parties), truly expanding the possibilities of medium format photography. Thus, if your photography falls outside the realm of standard equipment, you can very likely find a medium format camera to fit your needs.

Chapter 7

Making the Most of Medium Format

Working with medium format takes a different mindset than with a 35mm camera. Because you have 24 or 36 exposures with a 35mm camera, there is a tendency to click the shutter before actually considering the photograph you are taking. This is particularly noticeable with those using autofocus cameras. Because the camera works so quickly, the photographer often snaps the photo before truly considering what is in the frame. The result? More photos are taken, and fewer of them are decent shots.

The greatest advance in my photography came not from the photo class, which taught me proper technique, but from using an old Rolleicord and hand-held meter instead of my autofocus camera. Because the all-manual Rolleicord forced me to slow down, I took greater care in composition and was able to apply the techniques learned in class more fully.

"Working with medium format takes a different mindset than with a 35mm camera."

In this regard, medium format can also serve as a great teacher. Because it tends to be more technically demanding than 35mm, you will learn more about photography and how equipment works. As a result, those who use medium format for an extended period often see an improvement in all their photography—even if they ultimately chose to return to 35mm and never use medium format again.

□ Composition and Technique

Because the number of exposures is limited in comparison to 35mm, you need to take more care in composition. Pay attention to the film format, and compose to fit the negative.

This advice may seem a bit silly, but it is actually one of the greatest stumbling blocks when moving into medium format—particularly for 6x6 (square format) photographers. Too many photographers will shoot 6x6 expecting to crop down to a horizontal or vertical format in printing. As a result, they often overlook many excellent square images using the entire negative. With rectangular formats such as 6x7, it takes a little while to get used to shooting and printing, compared to 35mm. Not only is the 6x7 negative aspect ratio different (1:1.28 instead of the 1:1.5), but when printing an 8"x10" you will use virtually the entire negative (while a 35mm negative must be cropped to fit). Thus, your composition needs to be a bit tighter. Take care to make sure your composition is exactly what you want, and keep in mind that moving only a few feet can change a photograph tremendously, as seen in the photographs on the opposite page.

In 35mm, photographers often suggest that you bracket your important shots to ensure at least one good exposure. While I agree that bracketing important shots or images under difficult lighting is a good idea, due to the lower number of exposures per roll of film, bracketing every shot is not advisable. Additionally, bracketing is often used as an excuse not to learn proper metering technique. Consider the following—a 35mm photographer takes an entire roll of film, bracketing each photograph, and in the end, obtains twelve good images and tosses 24 bad exposures. A medium format photographer using proper metering took those same twelve shots, but on one roll of film without any frames wasted, and also reaps the benefit of larger negatives. To both

What a difference a few feet can make! I took these photos while walking along the Boulder Creek. I actually had to wade into the creek to get the shot, and the second shot was taken only a foot or two to the right of the first shot. When composing, small distances in camera position can often make or break a composition, so if you have the time, move around a bit to find the best shot.

improve your final images and reduce the need for bracketing, proper metering technique is required when using medium format.

My final word of advice on technique is to shoot loosely when necessary. In certain areas, such as sports and telephoto work, medium format simply does not have lenses available. As a result, take the image with your medium format camera and then crop the image when printing. Remember that in the worst case scenario, your cropped medium format negative will be the same quality as that of a 35mm negative. However, even cropped down, the medium format negative will offer better quality due to the increased negative area used in the final print.

☐ Buying Medium Format Equipment

When looking at medium format equipment, starting with a source like this book will often give you a good head start on what to look for and what types of equipment will best fit your needs. The next step is to actually find a medium format camera and buy it—which is easier said than done. Unlike with a 35mm SLR, you can't head down to the mall and find one. You need to find a good source of equipment, which means either finding a professional dealer with medium format equipment or scouring auctions, camera shows, etc., for used equipment.

In both cases, your best bet is to search out a good local camera dealer who sells both new and used equipment. Often, even local stores that sell only 35mm cameras new will have some used medium format cameras. Even if your local dealer doesn't carry any new or used medium format cameras, they will often know where you can find them and can give advice on which cameras to look for.

With medium format, it is also key to find a camera that fits your specific needs. In this regard, medium format is unlike 35mm. In general, most 35mm cameras (both current autofocus and older manual cameras) offer similar features and lens availability. However, in medium format, each camera or system has specific advantages over the others, and you need to make sure the camera you select meets your requirements.

The question of new versus used equipment is one of personal choice and budget. If you want the latest features or prefer new equipment, expect to pay at least $1000 for a new camera, and likely in the range of $2000–2500 for a complete camera system. Used equipment can often be found for less, but carries greater risk of mechanical failure or other problems. In either case, a good camera store will be able to help you find exactly what you're looking for.

Used Equipment. For many photographers entering medium format, buying new equipment simply isn't an option due to limited budgets. Used equipment can often be found at reasonable prices, but also comes with additional risk. Instead of receiving a factory warranty, you generally receive a thrity-day warranty on the equipment from most dealers. There may be no warranty at all from private sellers. Since it's used, there is a higher chance that something might go wrong with the equipment you have bought. Given this, you need to be careful when looking at used cameras.

"...you generally receive a thrity-day warranty on equipment from most dealers..."

The first item to consider is the overall condition of the equipment. The more brassing, scratches, dings, or dents, the more use or abuse the camera has seen. In many cases, outside appearance is a good indicator of mechanical condition—the more wear on the outside, the more wear on the inside. Thus, look for cameras that are in excellent condition cosmetically.

When looking at the lens, carefully inspect both the front and rear elemnts. If you find any flaws (spots, wipe marks, etc.), first have the seller clean the lens with lens cleaner and lens tissue. The majority of such marks are dirt on the lens, not flaws in the glass. If, after cleaning, the spots or marks still remain, there is definitely a flaw in the glass. Major scratches or chips on either the front or rear element can reduce image quality; damage to the rear element has far more impact. Hold the lens up to a light and look inside the lens. You should expect to see a little dust inside, but major amounts of dust or any damage to the internal elements will cause problems. Also look for haze or fungus (which sometimes looks like a spiderweb on an internal element), and do not buy a lens with these flaws. On lenses with leaf shutters, you may need to fire the shutter at B and hold it open to inspect the inner elements.

Also be sure to check all functions of the camera, including all shutter speeds. On early Rolleiflex cameras, for example, it is not uncommon for the slow speeds ($\frac{1}{15}$ second and slower) to be off or inoperative while the high speeds ($\frac{1}{30}$ second and up) are very accurate. This results from the lack of use of the slower speeds, not misuse or mechanical failure, and sometimes sticky leaf shutters may be cured simply by firing the shutter enough times to loosen the gummed-up lubricant. Often times, the camera simply needs a cleaning, lube, and adjustment—worth doing on a fine camera such as a Rollei, but not on an old folding camera or inexpensive TLR. Aside from the shutter, also make sure the film advance works properly. Take a test roll with the camera before you buy, if possible, to check alignment and spacing.

With all its pitfalls, used equipment can still be a great deal. Currently, all the equipment I use (35mm through large format) was purchased used or taken in trade. Granted, I have faced some repair bills that likely would never have occurred if I purchased new equipment, but I have done reasonably well overall. In buying used equipment, I do suggest you purchase your equipment from a reputable dealer to get a warranty (at least thirty days), and also to ensure the camera has been checked before it was put up for sale.

Of the used equipment I have bought, only one item that came from a dealer required repairs within thirty days of purchase. Two items I bought from private sellers had to go into the shop within thirty days. Private sellers also tend to be a bit more variable in the quality of used equipment they sell, while dealers will generally carry equipment that is in reasonable working order.

Numerical Rating System. The following guide is commonly used to rate used equipment.

[10]—The item is brand new and unused. All original packing, instruction books, accessories, and warranty cards are included.

[9+]—The item is brand new and unused. All original packing and accessories are included, but warranty cards or instruction books may be missing.

[9]—The item is used, but only a few times and it was well cared for. It may be in orignal packaging, but probably not. Optics and mechanics are perfect, and the equipment could be considered "like-new."

[9-]—The item is very lightly used. There may be one or two very minor cosmetic flaws, but the equipment looks almost like new. Optics and mechanics are perfect. *Note: Very little equipment on the market qualifies as 9- or higher. I have a hard time believing anyone, dealer or private seller, when they describe a piece of equipment in 9- or higher condition unless I have actually seen the equipment or a number of detailed photos. If you cannot see the camera before you buy it, consider any rating of 9- or higher inflated, and the equipment to actually be in 8 to 8+ condition.*

[8+]—The item is is above average condition. Equipment in this category was used lightly or was well cared for. It will be very clean, and have only a few minor cosmetic flaws. Optically and mechanically, it is perfect.

[8]—The item is in average condition (also called "excellent" on some scales). This equipment was used on a regular basis, and shows signs of use, but everything is still in excellent condition. Mechanically and optically, things are perfect. This is the condition most used equipment is in.

"With all its pitfalls, used equipment can still be a great deal..."

[8-]—This is equipment that has seen higher than average use, but is still in good condition. There will likely be some brassing and scratches, but nothing excessive. Mechanically and optically, the equipment should still be perfect.

[7+]—This is what I call "a good user." The equipment will show signs of heavy usage—brassing and scratches, but no dents. Optics are still excellent. Wipe marks are allowed, but there may be *no* major flaws such as deep scratches or chips. Mechanics must also be perfect. Something in this category may not look too pretty, but it still functions the way it should.

[7]—Cosmetically, the equipment shows signs of heavy usage—significant brassing, scratches, and maybe a few minor dents. Optically, there will be some scratches on the glass that may affect picture quality (but not too badly). Mechanically, the equipment must be in complete working order.

[7-]—The item is battered, but it still works. Mechanics must be fine, though they may not be

perfect (rough advance or some similar problem). There will be some noticeable optical or cosmetic flaws. All flaws must be clearly described.

[6]—It's ugly, but somehow the thing still functions. The equipment may need some repairs (broken meter, certain shutter speeds don't work, etc.), but it can still be used. All flaws must be clearly stated. Any camera in this condition will likely have a number of problems—scratched glass, dents, etc.

[5 or less]—This is a parts cameras, or one in need of major repairs. Known flaws should be stated, or the camera should be listed as inoperative.

Final Notes. Any camera with an engraved name or serial number cannot be considered any better than an 8-. From my experience, most used equipment falls into the 7+ to 8+ range, and very few pieces fall in the 9- or above category. Finally, no matter what condition the equipment is in, any and all flaws must be clearly stated before purchase or sale. When all else fails, I highly recommend using the ratings found in *Shutterbug* magazine as they are not as open to interpretation as a numerical system, and many people use the *Shutterbug* ratings as a standard for rating used equipment.

☐ Final Considerations

Darkroom Equipment. For those photographers with their own darkroom, a few changes or additions may be required. On the development side, most people with plastic tanks and adjustable reels are already equipped for medium format developing.

The development process is exactly the same as with 35mm film, and the only difference is learning to deal with the paper-backed films in medium format and getting the film onto the reel (it's a little trickier than with 35mm). Simply keep in mind that you can only do 120 film in standard plastic or stainless steel tanks. 220 film requires special tanks due to its long length.

In terms of chemicals and developer exhaustion, one roll of 120 film is equivilent to one roll of 36 exposures in 35mm, though you sometimes will need to put more chemicals in the tank to cover the taller 120 film.

For those developing and printing their own black and white negatives, the bottom line is clear. To process and print medium format negatives costs the same overall as 35mm. For most black and white

photographers with home darkrooms, only four to five negatives from each roll of film are usually printed—regardless of film format. Since film, chemicals, and paper cost virtually the same regardless of the camera used, there is very little difference in cost between 35mm and medium format. One trick often used by medium format photographers to keep costs low is to have film developed and get a contact sheet rather than prints. Then reprint or enlarge only the negatives you like. Not only does this cut down costs, but it also saves space. A sheet of negatives with contact sheet can be stored in a binder, while prints and loose negatives are harder to deal with.

"For photographers with their own darkroom, a few changes may be required."

For printing, you need to have an enlarger with light head large enough to cover your negative. Most medium format enlargers will cover up to 6x7, except for the Beseler 23C series enlargers which will also accommodate 6x9 negatives. An added bonus with medium format enlargers, is that they tend to be slightly larger and more rigid than smaller 35mm enlargers. This means you have greater stability and less potential for vibration problems, and you can also make larger prints.

Medium format also requires the use of different lenses sufficient to cover the negative size. In general, you need to use a lens that is the same focal length as the standard lens of the negative format you are printing. Thus, for 35mm negatives, you need a 50mm lens. 645 or 6x6 require a 75mm or 80mm lens, and 6x9 needs a 90mm or 105mm lens. In general, I recommend a modern lens to ensure contrast and sharpness, although you may not need to buy an APO lens unless you need the absolute highest quality or make extremely large prints (16"x20" or larger).

In all, working with medium format in a home darkroom is as easy as 35mm and equivalent in cost.

The Advantages of Medium Format

For the amateur, professional photographer, or weekend warrior, medium format should be seriously considered. With its larger negative and increased image quality, medium format offers a great deal to photographers looking for more than 35mm can provide, without jumping into large format. The portability and quality of medium format makes it suitable to a wide range of applications, from general photography to high-quality portraiture and technical photography. Also, contrary to popular belief, medium format film and processing often costs the same as a roll of 35mm, and quality equipment can often be purchased for less than the price of a new 35mm SLR.

People also tend to equate medium format with "serious" photography. As seen with those using fun and inexpensive folding cameras, Holgas, or old box cameras, this is certainly not always the case. Medium format can be as inexpensive as 35mm (and cheaper in some cases), and provide a great deal of fun and amusement. I carry an old folding camera with me often not because of the image quality, but because the camera and "guessposures" provide an excellent diversion. I find it an interesting challenge to see just what images I can produce using an old camera with no meter and "substandard" lens.

"The quality of medium format makes it suitable to a wide range of applications..."

In the end, anyone looking to improve their photography, or obtain professional quality results should seriously consider investing in a medium format camera. For general photography, the portability and improved image quality from larger negatives makes medium format a truly excellent option.

Glossary

ambient meter

Ambient meters measure the exact amount of light striking the subject, rather than the light bouncing off the subject. Because of this, ambient meters will not be fooled by excessively light or dark areas in your subject.

aspect ratio

The aspect ratio describes the proportions of a negative or print in terms of its width and height. This is expressed as a ratio (such a 1:1.5—the aspect ratio of a 35mm negative).

backlighting

A lighting situation where the main light source originates behind the subject. Backlighting requires special metering techniques in order to select the proper exposure.

ball heads (tripods)

A type of tripod head that allows a wide range of movements by adjusting only one screw. Many small ball heads cannot handle the weight of a medium format camera. For medium format cameras, buy at least a medium ball head.

barcode scanning

Just as 35mm film cassettes have DX coding to automatically set the film speed on the camera, medium format film manufacturers have started putting barcodes on the beginning of each film roll. Cameras equipped with barcode scanning can automatically set the film speed on the camera.

bayonet filter mount

A type of mount whereby a filter snaps into place, rather than screwing on.

bellows

A lighttight, flexible device mounted between the front and rear standards of certain types of cameras (most commonly field cameras, view cameras and older folding cameras). It serves to enclose the camera and prevent unwanted light from striking the film. It also allows the front or rear standard to be moved for focus or perspective control on field or view cameras.

bellows attachment

Lighttight, flexible device used to position the lens farther from the camera than normal to achieve greater magnification for macro and close-up photography.

box camera

An extremely simple camera that is really little more than a lighttight box, a lens, and a shutter. The Kodak Brownie and the Holga are examples of this type of camera.

bracketing

Shooting additional exposures that are less than and greater than the calculated correct exposure. This is done to help ensure that at least one frame will be properly exposed.

bubble levels (tripods)

A leveling device built into (or attached to) tripods to help the photographer accurately level the camera.

built-in meter

A light meter that comes installed in a camera. All built-in meters are reflected light meters.

center column (tripod)

The column, independent of the legs, onto which the camera is mounted. It can be raised and lowered for fine height adjustments.

contact array

The group of electronic contacts that allow the camera to communicate with the lens, film back or finder mounted on the camera. Found predominantly on later cameras offering electronic exposure control or other advanced electronic features.

contrast

The difference between the lightest and darkest areas in a print (or on a negative). By reducing unwanted light in the camera, coated lenses can improve contrast. Contrast can also be controlled in the darkroom, but only to a limited degree.

darkslide

A protective cover that is removed from a sheet film holder or film back when the film is to be exposed.

digital back

A type of back for interchangeable-back cameras that creates a digital image of a scene, rather than a negative.

enlarger

Device that projects light through a lens and a negative in order to expose the image on a piece of printing paper that is larger than the negative itself.

enlarging factor

Describes how much enlargement is required to make a negative cover the area of a given print size.

fall

The ability to lower the lens or film plane vertically. Used to make vertical lines appear parallel on film and for perspective control. (*See also* Rise.)

field camera

A type of camera that offers perspective control movements (such as rise, fall, tilt, shift), but these movements may be limited when compared to a view camera. (*See also* Standard *and* View camera.)

fill flash

The use of light from a flash to supplement existing light, rather than as the main light in a scene.

film back

Interchangeable film-holding (or digital capture) units that can be swapped and interchanged on a camera with an interchangeable back system. Allows the photographer to switch between shooting color, black and white, Polaroid®, different film speeds, etc., without having to rewind and reload the camera.

finder

The part of the camera through which the photographer composes and frames an image. Types of finders include prism, waist-level, and split-image rangefinder.

fisheye lens

A lens with an extremely short focal length that produces a very wide angle photograph. Photos taken with a fisheye lens display a characteristic distortion in the form of a bulging appearance that is most pronounced at the edges of the image.

flashmeter

A light meter specially designed to be able to meter the burst of light from a flash or group of flashes.

flash synchronization speed

The speed at which the shutter and the flash fire at precisely the same time and for the same duration.

flare

Unwanted light that reflects and scatters inside a lens and/or camera. Can cause loss of contrast.

focal length

The distance from the lens to the film plane, when the lens is focused on infinity. Greater focal lengths yield greater magnification.

focal plane shutter

A mechanism by which light is admitted to expose film through a moving opening (or slit) just in front of the film plane.

focusing helical

The rotating mount into which a lens is mounted so that it can be moved forward and backward for focusing. The alternative to focusing helicals is to use a bellows to focus, as seen on field and view cameras.

focusing screen

A piece of frosted glass, mounted in a camera, upon which the photographer views, composes, and focuses the image. On SLR and TLR cameras, the focusing screen is inside the finder. On field and view cameras, the focusing screen is located in the rear of the camera at the film plane.

geared head

A tripod head that uses gears, rather than locking knobs, to adjust the camera position. This allows extraordinarily precise control over camera positioning, but the gearing also makes these heads slow to work with. Very useful for technical photography where speed of operation is not a factor.

gray card

An card of 18% reflectance that can be used with a reflected light meter to determine proper exposure in a scene where no subject of "average" tone is available for metering.

hand grip

A "pistol" grip or other accessory grip designed to make handling the camera easier. Some hand grips also serve as motor drives or winders (such as Bronica's Speed Grip).

hand-held meter

A light meter that is a separate photographic instrument, rather than built into a camera.

image circle

The circle of usable light from a given lens. Within this circle, illumination will be even, with no falloff at the corners. The image circle will vary from lens to lens, and it an important factor in determining the amount of lens movement available on a view or field camera. The minimum image circle required for a film format is determined by the diagonal of the film, plus a few millimeters to ensure proper coverage (45mm on 35mm film, 75mm on 65 mm film, and 160mm on 4x5 film).

large format

Cameras that use film stock that is 4x5 or larger, usually in the form of individual sheets.

leaf shutter

A mechanism by which light is admitted to expose film by opening and closing a circular set of metal leaves mounted in the lens.

lens hood

A device that fits around a lens to prevent unwanted light from entering the camera.

load capacity (tripod)

The maximum amount of weight a tripod can handle before you run the risk of the tripod breaking. For tripods that have separate heads, be aware of the load capacity of the head as well as the tripod, and remember that the weight of the head counts against the maximum capacity of the tripod.

macro lens

A lens specifically designed for close-up photography and for reproducing images to exact scale on the negative.

medium format

Cameras that take film larger than 35mm, but smaller than large format.

middle gray

An 18% gray tone. Light meters provide an averaged reading for a subject based on this tone.

mirror lockup

A camera feature that allows the mirror to be moved and locked into position before an exposure is made. Eliminates vibration from mirror slap during the exposure.

mirror slap

In SLR cameras, mirror slap is the vibration caused by the movement of the camera's mirror during an exposure. This can affect the sharpness of the photograph.

motor drive

A camera feature or accessory that automatically advances the film after an exposure (unless overrides for multiple exposures are available).

movements

Controls (shift, tilt, rise and fall) in a camera or lens that allow the photographer to control perspective and depth of field. This is especially important in architectural photography, where lack of perspective control can result in distortion.

multicoated lens

A lens with multiple, highly advanced coatings on the glass that reduce internal reflections, flare, and the separation of colors as they pass through each lens element. Multiple lens coating (generally known as multicoating) improves transmittance of light through the lens element to 97–99.9%, depending on the manufacturer's formula and coating process. (*See also* Single-coated lens.)

OTF flashmetering

System for metering light from a flash off the film (OTF stands for "off the film").

panoramic camera

Camera equipped to create panoramic images (very wide angle images, normally with an aspect ratio between 1:2 and 1:3).

parallax

Because the finder on a TLR, rangefinder or viewfinder camera is separate from the actual taking lens (either above the taking lens, or above and to one side), what you see in the finder will not be exactly what is recorded on film by the taking lens. On a TLR this parallax error is only in the vertical orientation, but on viewfinder and rangefinder cameras, parallax error can be both vertical and horizontal in orientation. Generally, parallax is only a significant concern in situations where the subject is less than 15–20 feet away.

perspective control lenses

A lens designed with movements (shift, tilt, rise and fall) that allow the photographer to control perspective accurately. This is especially important in architectural photography, where lack of perspective control can result in distortion.

press cameras

This term generally refers to cameras, such as the Speed Graphic, which were commonly used in press photography through the 1950s. They are generally sheet film cameras resembling field cameras with very limited movements, and come in either 2¼x3¼ or 4x5 formats.

prism

Focusing directly off the focusing screen using a waist-level or vertical-chimney finder results in the photographer seeing a reversed image. A prism finder is one that reverses the image on the focusing screen so that you view and compose your image normally. Most prism finders are 90° finders (reflecting the image straight back at the photographer), but 45° finders, pentaprisms, porrofinders, rotating prisms, and other variations on the standard prism are also available for some systems.

quick-release

Rather that mounting the camera directly to the tripod head, it is mounted to a metal plate. This plate then snaps into place on the tripod head, allowing the camera to be quickly mounted and dismounted from the tripod.

rangefinder camera

A camera in which you frame your photograph through a finder separate from the taking lens, but not a matched lens as seen in the TLR design. Rangefinder cameras also feature the provision for focusing or parallax correction based on distance, hence the "range" in rangefinder. Most rangefinders include a coupled rangefinder, by which you can focus the lens. As you adjust the focus on the lens, you will see a double image in the viewfinder. When the two images meet and become a single image, the lens is in focus. This design is generally referred to as the split-image rangefinder, and is by far the most common. (*See also* Viewfinder Camera.)

red-window system

A camera with a clear red window on the back. This window allows the photographer to see the paper backing on 120 film. The numbers printed on the back of the film are then used to advance the film manually to the next frame.

reflective meter

A light meter that measures the amount of light reflected by a scene or subject. This is the type of meter installed in cameras (*See also* Built-in Meter).

resolution

The amount of information captured on a negative in relation to the size of the print made from it. The

more area (larger print) that the fixed amount of information on the negative must cover, the lower the resolution.

reversible center column

With certain tripods, you can reverse the center column so that the head (and camera) are attached below the tripod base. This allows you to place your camera closer to the ground and can be an advantage for macro photography, or in landscapes where you want to emphasize height.

rise

The ability to raise the lens or film plane vertically. Used to make vertical lines appear parallel on film and for perspective control. (*See also* Fall.)

sheet film adapter

A device that allows a camera that normally uses roll film to use sheet film instead.

shift

The ability to move the lens or film plane laterally. This provides perspective control to correct horizontal lines so that they appear parallel on film. On "tilt/shift" perspective control lenses for SLR cameras, the shift refers to the ability to shift the lens either horizontally or vertically.

single-coated lens

A lens with one coating on the glass that helps to reduce internal reflections, flare, and the separation of colors as they pass through each lens element. Single coating permits 90–95% or more of light to travel through each lens element rather than be reflected off the surface of the element, thus reducing flare and light loss. (*See also* Multicoated Lens.)

SLR camera

Using a mirror, a single lens reflex (SLR) camera allows the photographer to preview images through the same lens used to take the photograph, thus giving the ability to more precisely frame images.

split-image focusing

As you adjust the focus on the lens of a rangefinder camera, you see a double image in the viewfinder. When the two images meet and become a single image, the lens is in focus. This is referred to as split-image focusing.

spotmeter

A reflected light meter capable of taking precise readings of very small areas of a subject or scene.

standard (front or rear)

Refers to the front or back of a field or view camera. The front standard is where the lens attaches and the rear standard is where the film back or ground glass is attached.

sunny-16 rule

An outdoor exposure technique that does not require the use of a light meter. Under sunny conditions, it is calculated by the following equation: *Exposure = 1/(film speed) seconds at f16*. Since film speed rarely matches an actual shutter speed, use the closest possible shutter speed. Thus, if you are shooting a landscape with 100 speed film, your exposure would be $^1/_{125}$ second at f16.

taking lens

One TLR camera, the lens used to actually expose the film (i.e., "take" the picture). (*See also* TLR camera, *and* Parallax.)

technical camera

Cameras designed for specific technical applications, such as the Hasselblad MK-70 for photogrammetric survey, and the Linhof Aerotronica 69 for aerial photography.

telephoto lens

A lens with a very long focal length, and a reduced angle of view. Useful for photographing very distant or very small subjects.

thumb wheel

Dial used on some TLR cameras to adjust shutter speed and aperture.

tilt

The ability to tilt either the lens or film forwards or backwards. Used primarily for depth of field control.

TLR camera

A TLR (twin lens reflex) camera has two lenses. One is used for composing and focusing the image (the viewing lens), the other is used for making the actual exposure (the taking lens). (*See also* Parallax, Taking lens *and* Viewing lens.)

tripod head

The part of the tripod onto which the camera is attached.

TTL metering system

A metering system that reads light through the lens (TTL).

view camera

A type of camera offering tremendous control over depth of field and perspective through extensive camera movements (such as rise, fall, tilt and shift). Bellows mounted between the front and rear standards are used for focusing, and the image is com-

posed on a focusing screen mounted on the rear standard. Most often used in the studio for product photography and other applications where extensive movements are useful or necessary (including architectural photography). The size and weight of view cameras make them difficult to use in the field. (*See also* Field camera *and* Standard.)

viewfinder

A camera in which you frame your photograph through a finder separate from the taking lens, but not a matched lens as seen in the TLR design. (*See also* Rangefinder camera.)

viewing lens

On TLR cameras, the lens used to focus and frame the image. (*See also* TLR camera, *and* Parallax.)

waist-level viewfinder

A viewfinder that, rather than being raised to the eye to compose and focus images, is viewed from above (with the camera held closer to waist height).

wide-angle lens

A lens with a short focal length that provides a wider than normal view of a scene or subject.

winder

Device used to advance film to the next frame to be shot.

Zone System

A system of exposure, development and printing originally developed by Ansel Adams. It is based on the idea of breaking all the tones of the subject into ten Zones. Each Zone is one stop different from the next, with Zone V being middle gray (18% gray). Exposure is based on selecting a tone in the subject, and then choosing which Zone it should be placed into. Exposure can then be further adjusted for the contrast of the subject using N+1 or N-1 adjustments (N="normal," +/- refers to the number of stops of adjustment) for both exposure and development. It is a complicated system that takes time and practice to learn, but once mastered can be used to create negatives of consistently exceptional, repeatable and predictable quality.

zoom lens

A lens with multiple focal lengths that allows the user to reduce or enlarge the appearance of a scene without having to change the position of the camera.

Index

U

Underwater housings, 91
Used equipment
    cameras, 12, 65–66, 95–96
    condition, 94
    dealers vs. private sellers, 94
    lenses, 12–13, 94–96
    name brands, 13–14
    rating scales, 95
    testing, 94–95
    warranties, 94

V

Vibrations, 19
View cameras, 86–89
    models, 87–89
Viewfinder cameras, 52–63
    advantages and disadvantages, 52–53
    camera models, 54–63
    filters, 53
    lens design, 54
    parallax, 53
    portability, 53–54
    vs. viewfinders, 52

Vintage
    cameras, 11, 13, 94–96
    lenses, 12–13. 95–96

W

Warranties, 94–95
Weston Master meter, 63
Winders, 65

Y

Yashica TLRs, 49–50
    models, 49–50

Z

Zeiss
    box cameras, 57
    folding cameras, 56
Zoom lenses, 17

Other Books from
Amherst Media™

Build Your Own Home Darkroom

Lista Duren & Will McDonald

This classic book teaches you how to build a high quality, inexpensive darkroom in your basement, spare room, or almost anywhere. Includes valuable information on: darkroom design, woodworking, tools, and more! $17.95 list, 8½x11, 160p, 50 photos, many illustrations, order no. 1092.

Into Your Darkroom Step-by-Step

Dennis P. Curtin

This is the ideal beginning darkroom guide. Easy to follow and fully illustrated each step of the way. Includes information on: the equipment you'll need, set-up, making proof sheets and much more! $17.95 list, 8½x11, 90p, hundreds of photos, order no. 1093.

Camera Maintenance & Repair Book 1

Thomas Tomosy

An illustrated guide by a master camera repair technician. Includes: testing camera functions, general maintenance, basic tools and where to get them, basic repairs for accessories, camera electronics, plus "quick tips" for maintenance and more! $29.95 list, 8½x11, 176p, 100+ photos, order no. 1158.

Camera Maintenance & Repair Book 2

Thomas Tomosy

Build on the basics covered Book 1, with advanced techniques. Includes: mechanical and electronic SLRs, zoom lenses, medium format cameras, and more. Features models not included in the Book 1. $29.95 list, 8½x11, 176p, 150+ photos, charts, tables, appendices, index, glossary, order no. 1558.

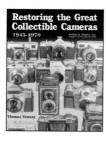

Restoring the Great Collectible Cameras (1945-70)

Thomas Tomosy

More step-by-step instruction on how to repair collectible cameras. Covers postwar models (1945-70). Hundreds of illustrations show disassembly and repair. $34.95 list, 8½x11, 128p, 200+ photos, index, order no. 1573.

Outdoor and Location Portrait Photography

Jeff Smith

Learn how to work with natural light, select locations, and make clients look their best. Step-by-step discussions and helpful illustrations teach you the techniques you need to shoot outdoor portraits like a pro! $29.95 list, 8½x11, 128p, 60+ b&w and color photos, index, order no. 1632.

Make Money with Your Camera

David Neil Arndt

Learn everything you need to know in order to make money in photography! David Arndt shows how to take highly marketable pictures, then promote, price and sell them. Includes all major fields of photography. $29.95 list, 8½x11, 120p, 100 b&w photos, index, order no. 1639.

Leica Camera Repair Handbook

Thomas Tomosy

A detailed technical manual for repairing Leica cameras. Each model is discussed individually with step-by-step instructions. Exhaustive photographic illustration ensures that every step of the process is easy to follow. $39.95 list, 8½x11, 128p, 130 b&w photos, appendix, order no. 1641.

Freelance Photographer's Handbook

Cliff & Nancy Hollenbeck

Whether you want to be a freelance photographer or are looking for tips to improve your current freelance business, this volume is packed with ideas for creating and maintaining a successful freelance business. $29.95 list, 8½x11, 107p, 100 b&w and color photos, index, glossary, order no. 1633.

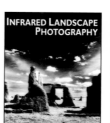

Infrared Landscape Photography

Todd Damiano

Landscapes shot with infrared can become breathtaking and ghostly images. The author analyzes over fifty of his most compelling photographs to teach you the techniques you need to capture landscapes with infrared. $29.95 list, 8½x11, 120p, 60 b&w photos, index, order no. 1636.

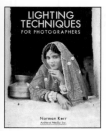

Lighting Techniques for Photographers

Norman Kerr

This book teaches you to predict the effects of light in the final image. It covers the interplay of light qualities, as well as color compensation and manipulation of light and shadow. $29.95 list, 8½x11, 120p, 150+ color and b&w photos, index, order no. 1564.

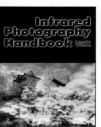

Infrared Photography Handbook

Laurie White

Covers black and white infrared photography: focus, lenses, film loading, film speed rating, batch testing, paper stocks, and filters. Black & white photos illustrate how IR film reacts. $29.95 list, 8½x11, 104p, 50 b&w photos, charts & diagrams, order no. 1419.

How to Shoot and Sell Sports Photography

David Arndt

A step-by-step guide for amateur photographers, photojournalism students and journalists seeking to develop the skills and knowledge necessary for success in the demanding field of sports photography. $29.95 list, 8½x11, 120p, 111 photos, index, order no. 1631.

How to Operate a Successful Photo Portrait Studio

John Giolas

Combines photographic techniques with practical business information to create a complete guide book for anyone interested in developing a portrait photography business (or improving an existing business). $29.95 list, 8½x11, 120p, 120 photos, index, order no. 1579.

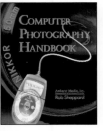

Computer Photography Handbook

Rob Sheppard

Learn to make the most of your photographs using computer technology! From creating images with digital cameras, to scanning prints and negatives, to manipulating images, you'll learn all the basics of digital imaging. $29.95 list, 8½x11, 128p, 150+ photos, index, order no. 1560.

Achieving the Ultimate Image

Ernst Wildi

Ernst Wildi teaches the techniques required to take world class, technically flawless photos. Features: exposure, metering, the Zone System, composition, evaluating an image, and more! $29.95 list, 8½x11, 128p, 120 b&w and color photos, index, order no. 1628.

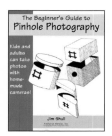

The Beginner's Guide to Pinhole Photography

Jim Shull

Take pictures with a camera you make from stuff you have around the house. Develop and print the results at home! Pinhole photography is fun, inexpensive, educational and challenging. $17.95 list, 8½x11, 80p, 55 photos, charts & diagrams, order no. 1578.

Telephoto Lens Photography

Rob Sheppard

A complete guide for telephoto lenses. Shows you how to take great wildlife photos, portraits, sports and action shots, travel pics, and much more! Features over 100 photographic examples. $17.95 list, 8½x11, 112p, b&w and color photos, index, glossary, appendices, order no. 1606.

Restoring Classic & Collectible Cameras (Pre-1945)

Thomas Tomosy

Step-by-step instructions show how to restore a classic or vintage camera. Repair mechanical and cosmetic elements to restore your valuable collectibles. $34.95 list, 8½x11, 128p, 175 photos and illus., glossary, index, order no. 1613.

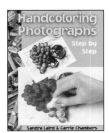

Handcoloring Photographs Step-by-Step

Sandra Laird & Carey Chambers

Learn to handcolor photographs step-by-step with the new standard in handcoloring reference books. Covers a variety of coloring media and techniques with plenty of colorful photographic examples. $29.95 list, 8½x11, 112p, 100+ color and b&w photos, order no. 1543.

Special Effects Photography Handbook

Elinor Stecker-Orel

Create magic on film with special effects! Little or no additional equipment required, use things you probably have around the house. Step-by-step instructions guide you through each effect. $29.95 list, 8½x11, 112p, 80+ color and b&w photos, index, glossary, order no. 1614.

McBroom's Camera Bluebook, *6th Edition*

Mike McBroom

Comprehensive and fully illustrated, with price information on: 35mm, digital, APS, underwater, medium & large format cameras, exposure meters, strobes and accessories. Pricing info based on equipment condition. A must for any camera buyer, dealer, or collector! $29.95 list, 8½x11, 336p, 275+ photos, order no. 1553.

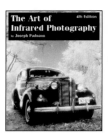

The Art of Infrared Photography, *4th Edition*

Joe Paduano

A practical guide to the art of infrared photography. Tells what to expect and how to control results. Includes: anticipating effects, color infrared, digital infrared, using filters, focusing, developing, printing, handcoloring, toning, and more! $29.95 list, 8½x11, 112p, 70 photos, order no. 1052

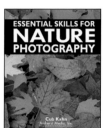

Essential Skills for Nature Photography

Cub Kahn

Learn all the skills you need to capture landscapes, animals, flowers and the entire natural world on film. Includes: selecting equipment, choosing locations, evaluating compositions, filters, and much more! $29.95 list, 8½x11, 128p, 60 photos, order no. 1652.

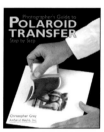

Photographer's Guide to Polaroid Transfer

Christopher Grey

Step-by-step instructions make it easy to master Polaroid transfer and emulsion lift-off techniques and add new dimensions to your photographic imaging. Fully illustrated every step of the way to ensure good results the very first time! $29.95 list, 8½x11, 128p, 50 photos, order no. 1653.

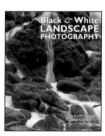

Black & White Landscape Photography

John Collett and David Collett

Master the art of b&w landscape photography. Includes: selecting equipment (cameras, lenses, filters, etc.) for landscape photography, shooting in the field, using the Zone System, and printing your images for professional results. $29.95 list, 8½x11, 128p, 80 b&w photos, order no. 1654.

Photo Retouching with Adobe® Photoshop®

Gwen Lute

Designed for photographers, this manual teaches every phase of the process, from scanning to final output. Learn to restore damaged photos, correct imperfections, create realistic composite images and correct for dazzling color. $29.95 list, 8½x11, 120p, 60+ photos, order no. 1660.

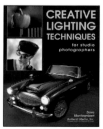

Creative Lighting Techniques for Studio Photographers

Dave Montizambert

Master studio lighting and gain complete creative control over your images. Whether you are shooting portraits, cars, table-top or any other subject, Dave Montizambert teaches you the skills you need to confidently create with light. $29.95 list, 8½x11, 120p, 80+ photos, order no. 1666.

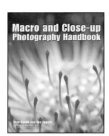

Macro and Close-up Photography Handbook

Stan Sholik

Learn to get close and capture breathtaking images of small subjects – flowers, stamps, jewelry, insects, etc. Designed with the 35mm shooter in mind, this is a comprehensive manual full of step-by-step techniques. $29.95 list, 8½x11, 120p, 80 photos, order no. 1686.

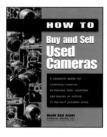

How to Buy and Sell Used Cameras

David Neil Arndt

Learn the skills you need to evaluate the cosmetic and mechanical condition of used cameras, and buy or sell them for the best price possible. Also learn the best places to buy/sell and how to find the equipment you want. $19.95 list, 8½x11, 112p, b&w, 60 photos, order no. 1703.

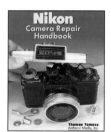

Nikon Camera Repair Handbook

Thomas Tomosoy

Nikon cameras have come to epitomize the camera collector's dream. From body to lenses to internal mechanics and accessories, this book shows the reader how to repair, restore and maintain Nikon equipment. $39.95 list, 8½x11, 144p, 225 b&w photos, order no. 1707.

AMHERST MEDIA'S CUSTOMER REGISTRATION FORM

Please fill out this sheet and send or fax to receive free information about future publications from Amherst Media.

CUSTOMER INFORMATION

DATE

NAME

STREET OR BOX #

CITY   STATE

ZIP CODE

PHONE (   )

OPTIONAL INFORMATION

I BOUGHT *Medium Format Cameras* BECAUSE

I FOUND THESE CHAPTERS TO BE MOST USEFUL

I PURCHASED THE BOOK FROM

City   State

I WOULD LIKE TO SEE MORE BOOKS ABOUT

I PURCHASE   BOOKS PER YEAR

ADDITIONAL COMMENTS

FAX to: 1-800-622-3298

CUT ALONG DOTTED LINE

if mailing, fold in number order along dashed lines.

Name_____
Address_____
City_____State_____
Zip_____ — _____

Place
Postage
Here

Amherst Media, Inc.
PO Box 586
Amherst, NY 14226

if mailing, paste underside of flap, or tape here.